Harrap's Agenda Business English through Case Studies

Workbook

Harrap's Agenda Business English through Case Studies

Workbook

David Cotton and Roger Owen

Harrap London

First published in Great Britain 1980
by HARRAP LIMITED
19–23 Ludgate Hill, London EC4M 7PD

Reprinted : 1982 (twice); 1983; 1987

© David Cotton and Roger Owen 1982, 1980

All rights reserved. No part of this
publication may be reproduced in any
form or by any means without the prior
permission of Harrap Limited

ISBN: 0 245–53347–8

Illustrations by Ray Fishwick
Cover by Brooke Calverley

NOTE
All the places, characters and incidents in
this book are entirely fictitious and bear no
relation whatsoever to any known person,
firm or company.

Acknowledgements

We should like to thank the following:
A.E.C. Electric Fencing Ltd for their help and
cooperation; Hitachi Sales (UK) for permission
to reproduce material from one of their brochures
(p. 114); Institute of Export for permission to
reproduce an excerpt from Specimen Agency
Agreement for Exporters (pp. 98–9); Japan Air
Lines for permission to reproduce an extract from
their timetables (p. 75).

Printed and bound in Great Britain by
Henry Ling Ltd, Dorchester.

CONTENTS

HOW TO USE THIS BOOK	7
BONHOMME	11
CHAIRS	16
ELITE	21
FUNFABBRIX	26
JCS	31
WATCHMERE	36
GIORDANO	42
COCONUT GROVE	47
TUMBRIL	52
HI-FLITE	57
BARNWOOD	62
EASY GO	67
MACQUILTER	73
WESTMEATH	79
TANSKIN	85
BLIK	91
KRETEK	96
CARBONIDE	101
AFJUZ	107
KYOSEC	112
APPENDIX: EXAMPLES OF BUSINESS WRITING	119
Section 1 A business letter	120
2 An inter-office memo	122
3 A telex message	124
4 A short report	125

HOW TO USE THIS BOOK

For a general description of Agenda, see the preface to the Casebook.

WORKBOOK

This Workbook provides comprehensive language practice to go with each case study in Agenda Casebook. All the Workbook units follow the same pattern. Each unit contains the following:

Understanding the case The purpose of the comprehension questions is to make students think about the case study and its problems in depth – to encourage problem analysis.

Vocabulary Each exercise is centred on the vocabulary of a particular topic area.

Dialogue, functions and role-playing exercises The dialogue, which is recorded on the accompanying tapes, is intended for listening practice. It will accustom the student to a variety of accents and a wide range of styles of speech – from the formal to the colloquial. Each dialogue also contains examples of different ways of expressing a particular function, and the most useful structures used for this are shown in a list following the dialogue. A role-playing exercise gives advanced students the opportunity to use these structures in an imaginary situation.

Numeracy exercise This is intended to give students practice in talking about numbers, statistics, diagrams, spatial relationships and so on.

The right words in the right place This is a register transfer exercise: the student is given practice in turning one kind of English into another – for example, in 'translating' the formal terms of an agreement into the more colloquial English of a telephone conversation.

Written assignment There are two of these for each unit. The emphasis is on memoranda, telex messages and report writing, as these are less fully dealt with in standard textbooks than business letters; there are, however, a number of letter-writing exercises. In each unit, one assignment is analysed in detail so that the less confident student is helped to carry it out successfully. Notes on the commonest types of business document (letter, memo, telex and report), with an example of each, are given in the Appendix to this Workbook.

Idioms section A number of colloquial expressions are given at the end of each unit. Some are in general use, others are peculiar to businessmen. The foreign speaker need not necessarily be able to use them all in an active way, but should be able to understand them when he or she hears them.

CASSETTES/TAPES

Recorded tapes accompany this Workbook and contain all the Workbook dialogues plus fluency drills based on functional structures and phrases taken from the dialogue. Although many of the speakers are native English-speakers (including regional accents), a good variety of non-native accents can also be heard, since it is obviously important in business to be able to understand one's opposite number from France, Japan or Brazil. The structures, vocabulary and usages, however, are those of standard English throughout – normally British English, though some American English has been used where appropriate.

APPENDIX: EXAMPLES OF BUSINESS WRITING

The Appendix to the Workbook contains examples of a letter, a memo, a telex and a report, with notes on the layout and content of each. These can be used for instruction or for reference, and will give basic guidance in handling the written assignments in each unit.

BOOK OF ANSWERS (Teacher's Book)

This book contains:
- an outline of the pros and cons of each suggested course of action in the Casebook
- suggested answers to Workbook comprehension questions
- a key to Workbook vocabulary exercises
- notes on numeracy exercises
- suggested answers to register transfer exercises
- notes on idioms
- transcript of the material recorded on the tapes.

Work scheme A (Workbook exercises after group discussion)

CASEBOOK
Private study/group study
of Casebook text
↓
WORKBOOK (Oral)
'Understanding the case'
(Comprehension questions)
↓
CASEBOOK
Problem analysis:
informal group discussion
↓
Preliminary meetings
↓
GROUP DISCUSSION AND
DECISION-MAKING
↓
Post mortem
↓
WORKBOOK (Oral)
Vocabulary exercise
↓
Dialogue work
↓
Functional practice
↓
Role-play
↓
Numeracy exercise
↓
WORKBOOK (Written)
'The right words in the
right place'
(Register transfer exercise)
↓
'Written assignment(s)'
↓
The final section in each unit can be studied at any time.

Work scheme B (Workbook exercises before group discussion)

CASEBOOK
Private study/group study
of Casebook text
↓
WORKBOOK (Oral)
'Understanding the case'
(Comprehension questions)
↓
Vocabulary exercise
↓
CASEBOOK
Problem analysis:
informal group discussion
↓
WORKBOOK (Oral)
Dialogue work
↓
Functional practice
↓
Role-play
↓
Numeracy exercise
↓
CASEBOOK
Preliminary meetings
↓
GROUP DISCUSSION AND
DECISION-MAKING
↓
Post mortem
↓
WORKBOOK (Written)
'The right words in the
right place'
(Register transfer exercise)
↓
'Written assignment(s)'
↓
The final section in each unit can be studied at any time.

UNDERSTANDING THE CASE

Read the case study in the Casebook and answer these questions.

1. What positions do these people hold?
   (i) Carlson Overend Junior   (ii) Jacques Duperrier   (iii) Jean Pinot
2. Compare, in terms of size only, the Brant Corporation and Bonhomme.
3. What is the relationship between the two companies?
4. Why did Carlson Overend decide to meet Bonhomme's senior executives?
5. How do you think the executives were feeling before Overend arrived?
6. What was probably the turning point in that meeting?
7. What are some of the positive and negative effects on Bonhomme of the Brant takeover?
8. To determine English language needs, Bonhomme personnel were asked to assess their own proficiency on a four-point scale. How accurate and valid do you think such assessments can be?
9. What strikes you as significant when you examine the results in the charts taken from Pinot's report?
10. What do you think would be the major difficulties in setting up any kind of English language training scheme for Bonhomme?

VOCABULARY Who works for Bonhomme?

Jean Pinot reviews the language problem in his company. Fill in the gaps in his remarks from the box below. There may be more than one possible choice. Not all the words in the list need be used. You may have to change the ending of a word, for example, to indicate the tense of a verb or to show that a noun is plural.

Pinot We have a total w___f___ of about six hundred and fifty. About thirty per cent of the company's _____ are office _____, employed at our headquarters in Paris. A___(a)___ more are located in Lille, where we have a small factory, and all the rest are engaged in overseas projects. We have very ___(a)___ unskilled _____ on the p___r___, because it's our p_____ to employ local l_____ on a temporary basis as and when we need it. However, that makes our industrial t_____ problems all the greater. The work our people do is highly s_____, and at a very advanced l_____.

You can see how this will affect our language programme, especially since most of our _____ speak very _____ English at the moment. The B_____ of D_____ aren't much good and the s_____ e_____ are no better. J_____ m_____ seem to be the best. Duperrier, the _____, has a P_____ A_____ who's bilingual. But she's half-English, anyway.

2 employee	assistant	(a) few
7 labour	board	(a) little
5 payroll	director	
6 personal	executive	10 level
4 personnel	junior	policy
staff	management	9 specialized
3 worker	manager	8 training
1 workforce	managing	
	president	
	senior	

LANGUAGE TRAINING—DISCUSSING THE OPTIONS

Read or listen to the dialogue.

Jean Pinot, Jacques Duperrier and Susan Sharp, a business colleague from the UK, are discussing possible solutions to the problem of language training.

Susan But tell me, Jacques, does Overend really want everyone here to learn English?

Duperrier Not everyone, of course, but let's face it, a lot of our people already have to use English in their work, and in the future that number's going to increase.

Susan Couldn't you wait a few months and see how things go?

Duperrier That's just not possible, Susan. People from the States will be coming over here soon, and don't forget, Brant are going to have a big sales drive with Bonhomme in North America. They plan to use some of our people for that. No, we need to set up a big training programme now. What's your view, Jean?

Pinot Well . . . I suggest we start by selecting a few executives for some on-the-spot training. We can be more ambitious later.

Duperrier Oh no, I really can't agree with you there, Jean. I just don't like half-measures. If we're going to do something, let's do it properly—even if it is expensive.

Susan You know, I think it would be a good idea if you contacted the British International Advisory Council. After all, English teaching is their speciality.

Pinot Yes, that's certainly worth considering. But let's look at all the angles. Another point is—and this may be more important than you think—there's British English and American English. They're not the same, as you know.

Susan Right. Well, in that case, how about calling the New Horizon Study Center? They're near to you and the owner's American. Some of our staff from the Paris office have been there and found it reasonable.

Duperrier Yes, that's a good idea. Well, obviously we must approach this problem systematically. Perhaps Jean could make a start for us by looking into all the possibilities.

1 Listen again and find as many expressions as possible which are used to suggest a course of action.
2 Practise the expressions recorded after the dialogue on the tape.
3 With the following check-list to help you, do the role-playing exercise.

SUGGESTING A COURSE OF ACTION

Couldn't you . . . ?

I suggest we . . .

Let's . . .

I think it would be a good idea if . . .

How about ———ing . . . ?

Perhaps you could . . .

Why don't we . . . ?

Can't we . . . ?

Role-playing exercise

If necessary, which rooms on Bonhomme's premises could be used for English language classes? Duperrier and his Personal Assistant are discussing this question with Jean Pinot and the English Language Training Adviser. They make several suggestions, but Pinot and the Adviser object to each of them.

These are the locations proposed by Duperrier and his assistant:

— a room outside the staff canteen (6 square metres)

— the present rest room of the factory workers

— one of the luxurious conference rooms (10 metres by 12 metres)

— a room at the top of the administration block, above the typing and photocopying centre.

ARE EXPORTS REALLY NECESSARY?

The graphs and figures below are taken from Bonhomme's annual report for 1989–90 (1990 figures are reliable estimates). Study this evidence carefully and consider possible answers to the questions.

GEOGRAPHICAL ANALYSIS

Profit $.000	Turnover $m	Overseas
781	4.31	North Africa
1,640	8.98	Middle East
−713 (loss)	1.36	Canada
952	2.37	Europe
2,660	17.02	
2,076	13.54	France
4,736	30.56	

Pre-tax Profits

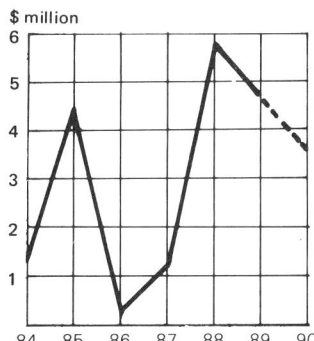

Exports

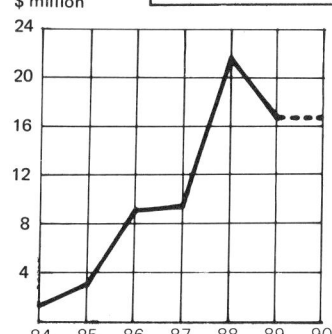

Turnover

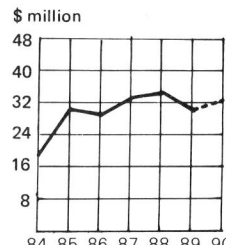

1 Expressing your answers as approximate percentages, compare
  (a) turnover in 1988 and 1989
  (b) turnover in 1984 and 1990.

2 What strikes you as significant when you compare exports and turnover throughout the six-year period?

3 How big a contribution do exports make to Bonhomme's profits? Is overseas business likely to become more important or less important?

4 Which year, in your opinion, witnessed the most decisive change in Bonhomme's fortunes?

THE RIGHT WORDS IN THE RIGHT PLACE

We need to be able to say the same thing in different ways. The words we use in chatting to a friend may not be suitable at a meeting, in the Managing Director's office, on the telephone, or in a letter.

> Here are six ways in which people might express fairly strong opinions, in a very informal situation. In the example, you can see how employees rephrase their remarks when they talk to the boss. Rewrite the other remarks in the same way.

Example
  'How on earth does Overend think all these people are going to learn English so fast? It's crazy!'
  'Mr Overend, don't you think it's a little unreasonable to expect Bonhomme staff to learn English in such a short time?'

1 'I guess Overend is going to have to put his money where his mouth is and buy a language laboratory.'
  'Might I suggest, Mr Overend, . . .?'

2 'Well, if you ask me, if you've got to learn a language, you can't beat going to the place where they speak it.'

3 'Ah, but don't forget that a language laboratory on its own is no use to anyone. You've got to have people to run it; you've got to have a full-scale training programme, and there are all sorts of bits and pieces that go with it.'

4 'Quite honestly, I think so far everyone's been talking rubbish. Nobody seems to realize how big this problem is.'

5 'It's perfectly obvious what we should do! Get these New Horizon people to handle it—they're supposed to be the professionals in this game, after all.'

WRITTEN ASSIGNMENT

> Carlson Overend has asked Jacques Duperrier to send a memo to Brant's Director of Personnel in Chicago. Its purpose is to give details of the language training problem at Bonhomme and to outline the proposals now being considered to improve the language skills of the staff. Draft this memo for Duperrier.

PRESENTATION

Lay out and address your memo correctly. There is an example of how to do this in the Appendix, section 2.

Give the memo a title. This must say exactly what the memo is about. A good way of inventing a title is to state what general area or activity the memo refers to (e.g. *Staff training*) and then to say what part of that area is particularly concerned (e.g. *Proposals for English language training*).

HOW TO START

Say why the memo is being written, and what topics it deals with.

I am writing at the request of Mr Overend . . .
I have been asked to inform you about . . .
This memo concerns the problem of . . .

OUTLINING THE SITUATION

Select and summarize only the most important facts.

The situation is as follows: . . .
The problem is . . .
Action is necessary for the following reasons: . . .

In this section of your memo, you may decide to include some statistics taken from the charts given in the Casebook.

GIVING INFORMATION

The Director of Personnel is mainly interested at the moment in knowing what suggestions have been made regarding language training. No decisions are required from him at this point. It is, therefore, only necessary to list the four proposals finally presented by Pinot.

The following proposals are now under discussion: . . .
A number of suggestions are receiving consideration: . . .
A full investigation is being made into the following possibilities: . . .

You will probably want to tabulate the suggestions and present them as a list of numbered items. Remember that each item in the list should be expressed by means of the same grammatical pattern. Here are two possible ways of presenting such a list:

The following proposals are now under discussion:
(a) to take no immediate action
(b) to set up a limited in-house training programme
(c) to contact the British International Advisory Council
(d) to get information about courses from a language school.

In the list above, every item begins with an infinitive construction. In the following example, every item begins with a *that* clause.

The following proposals are now under discussion:
(a) that no immediate action should be taken
(b) that a limited in-house training scheme should be set up
(c) that the British International Advisory Council should be contacted
(d) that information about courses should be obtained from a language school.

CONCLUDING

This is a short, simple memo, which is meant only to inform. There is no need for any conclusion at all; the formal courtesies used to conclude a business letter would be out of place in a memo. There is no formal signature either, just your initials.

Additional assignment

Imagine you are Jean Pinot. Write a letter, either to the New Horizon Study Center or to the Swedish electronics company, asking for details of their services and their terms of business.

HEARD IN THE CORRIDOR

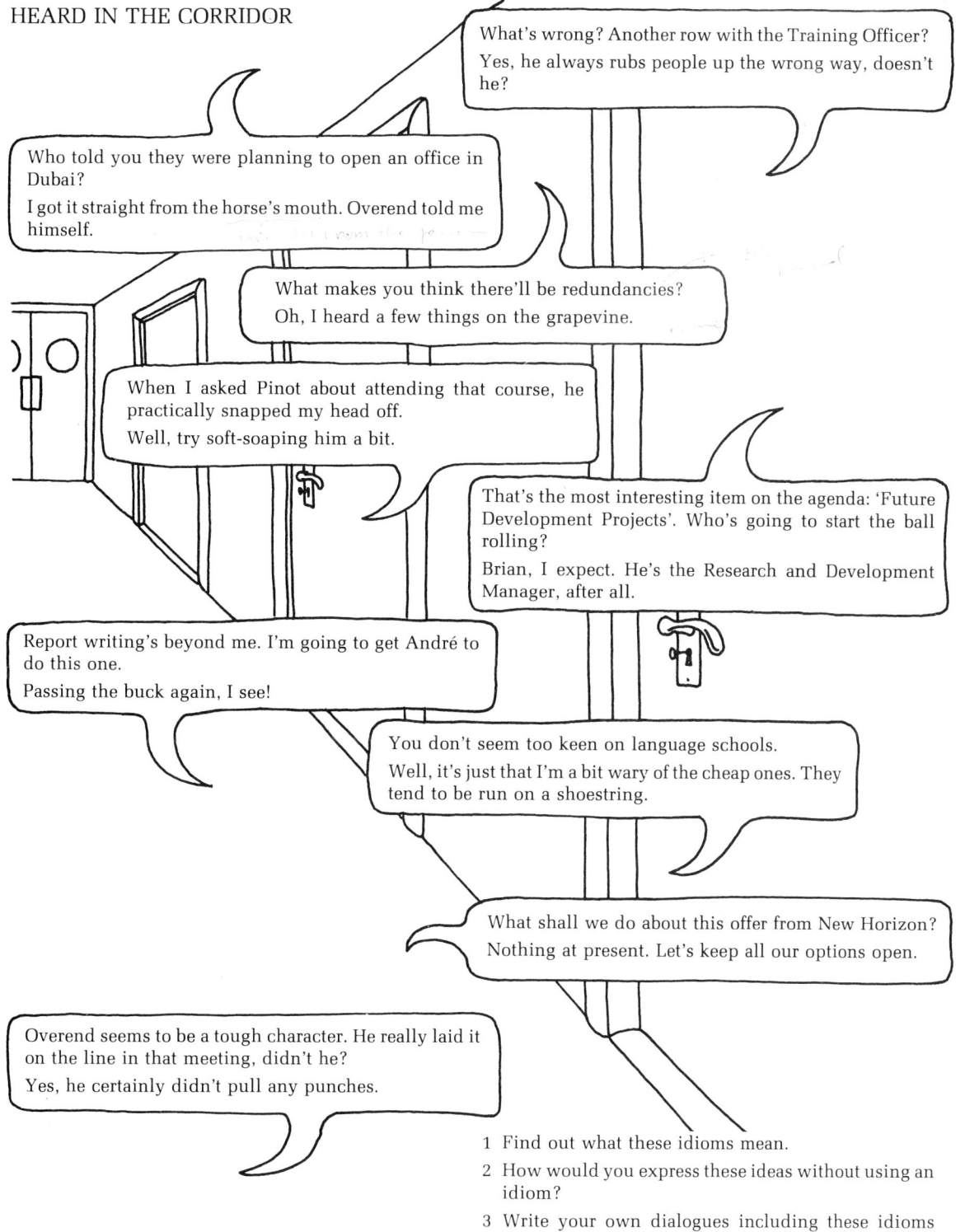

What's wrong? Another row with the Training Officer?
Yes, he always rubs people up the wrong way, doesn't he?

Who told you they were planning to open an office in Dubai?
I got it straight from the horse's mouth. Overend told me himself.

What makes you think there'll be redundancies?
Oh, I heard a few things on the grapevine.

When I asked Pinot about attending that course, he practically snapped my head off.
Well, try soft-soaping him a bit.

That's the most interesting item on the agenda: 'Future Development Projects'. Who's going to start the ball rolling?
Brian, I expect. He's the Research and Development Manager, after all.

Report writing's beyond me. I'm going to get André to do this one.
Passing the buck again, I see!

You don't seem too keen on language schools.
Well, it's just that I'm a bit wary of the cheap ones. They tend to be run on a shoestring.

What shall we do about this offer from New Horizon?
Nothing at present. Let's keep all our options open.

Overend seems to be a tough character. He really laid it on the line in that meeting, didn't he?
Yes, he certainly didn't pull any punches.

1 Find out what these idioms mean.
2 How would you express these ideas without using an idiom?
3 Write your own dialogues including these idioms correctly and appropriately used.

UNDERSTANDING THE CASE

Read the case study in the Casebook and answer these questions.

1. What position does Dudley Morris hold?
2. What do we know about the university in which he works?
3. How has the job changed for Dudley Morris since he first became Chief Purchasing Officer?
4. What evidence is there that the Finance Officer did not 'beat about the bush' when he phoned Dudley Morris?
5. The Dean of the Arts faculty and the Students' Union President do not entirely agree about the function of the Common Room. How do they differ?
6. What do you think should be the function of a Students' Common Room?
7. What do we know about the floor of the Common Room, and how might this information influence our choice of a suitable set of chairs for it?
8. What criteria should be used to choose the most suitable chairs?
9. Are there any other items of furniture or equipment which you think students might wish to add to the Common Room in the future?
10. Do you have any ideas concerning a suitable décor for the Common Room, for example, colour and type of ceiling, lighting system?

VOCABULARY **What sort of chairs?**

The President of the Students' Union is reflecting on the meeting he has just attended at which Morris presented the types of chairs available. Fill in the gaps in his remarks from the box below. There may be more than one possible choice. Not all the words in the list need be used. You may have to change the ending of a word, for example, to indicate the tense of a verb or to show that a noun is plural.

President Poor old Dudley! He's just r_____ that his b_____ for buying Common Room furniture has been _____ in half. I can a_____ how he feels. But we're not going to l_____ our standards. We must _____ on decent furniture.

For a b_____ o_____ like this the supplier ought to give us a pretty generous d_____, or simply r_____ the price.

The committee originally s_____ hardwood f_____s, foam rubber p_____ and good-quality c_____. We didn't want any of these man-made fibres. There's no s_____ for wool, or maybe cotton.

I don't mind m_____-p_____ furniture, though. It's easier to r_____ if it wears out or gets smashed up.

Those leather armchairs cost twice _____ anything else, but I bet you they'll last a lot longer. They're h_____-m_____ out of first-rate m_____. Actually, per person, the big leather sofas only cost about ten per cent _____ the plastic chairs. Perhaps we could get them re-covered. Could someone ask for a(n) _____?

appreciate	cloth	as much as
realize	cover	more than
understand	frame	
	material	insist
budget	padding	specify
discount		
estimate	bulk order	
quotation	hand-made	
cut	mass-produced	
lower	substitute	
reduce		
replace		

A DISCUSSION ABOUT FURNITURE

Read or listen to the dialogue.

Dudley Morris is talking to Dick Makepiece and Patricia McNee, the President and Vice-President of the Students' Union.

Makepiece I think we'd all agree, Mr Morris, that the chairs have got to be sturdy. They're bound to get some rough treatment from time to time.

Morris Yes. They'll need to be solid all right. Good strong frames. Hardwood perhaps, or beech. And the covers would have to be made of a really tough material. Another thing, I think it's essential that the chairs should be fairly compact.

McNee Right. We mustn't forget that the Common Room isn't that big. But, you know, one thing no one's mentioned is design. We should try to find something that has nice lines, something with style, even if it's a bit jazzy.

Morris Well . . . I'll do my best, but that sort of thing can cost the earth, as you well know. Let's forget about the chairs for a moment. What about the coffee tables? Any ideas?

Makepiece I prefer round tables to oblong or square.

McNee I quite agree, Dick. Round tables don't take up so much room, and when you're in a big group, it's easier to talk across them. I wonder what colour they should be.

Morris Well, if we buy the chairs in bulk, the supplier will probably be able to offer us a matching coffee table. But you know, there is one problem. I'd like the tables to have heat-resistant tops.

Makepiece Really? That would be expensive, wouldn't it?

Morris But worth it. People will drop anything on coffee tables, believe me. Lighted cigarettes, hot coffee . . .

McNee Oh dear, the longer we go on talking, the less certain I am we'll get what we want. The chairs have got to be strong, compact and fashionable, the tables must be round, heat-resistant and match the chairs . . .

Morris And above all, the price has got to be right!

1. Listen again and find as many expressions as possible which are used to state requirements.
2. Practise the expressions recorded after the dialogue on the tape.
3. With the following check-list to help you, do the role-playing exercise.

STATING YOUR REQUIREMENTS

It's got to be . . .
They'll need to be . . .
It would have to be . . .
I think it's essential that . . .
We should try to . . .
I'd like X to . . .
It must be . . .
It's vital/important that . . .
Ideally, they should be . . .
What we want is . . .

Role-playing exercise

A new students' residence is to be built next year. It will comprise eighty single study bedrooms. Members of the university's Planning Committee (including the Chancellor and Finance Officer) are discussing the project with a group of students. They want to find out exactly what kind of study bedroom the students require. For example, what should be its dimensions? What décor should it have? How should it be furnished? What equipment should be installed? What about lighting and heating?

A BIT OF A SQUEEZE?

The Students' Union Planning Committee proposes that the new Common Room should be divided into 'activity areas' as follows:

(a) a coffee-drinking area

(b) a corner for card-players (8 or 12 persons)

(c) a chess-playing area (4 small tables)

(d) space for a table for newspapers and periodicals

(e) an area for conversation and seminars

(f) an open space for exhibitions; this should be easily cleared for dancing or parties

(g) space for playing darts (this game requires a board, hung on a blank wall; the player stands about 2.5 metres from the board)

Study the floor plan of the Common Room and consider the questions below it.

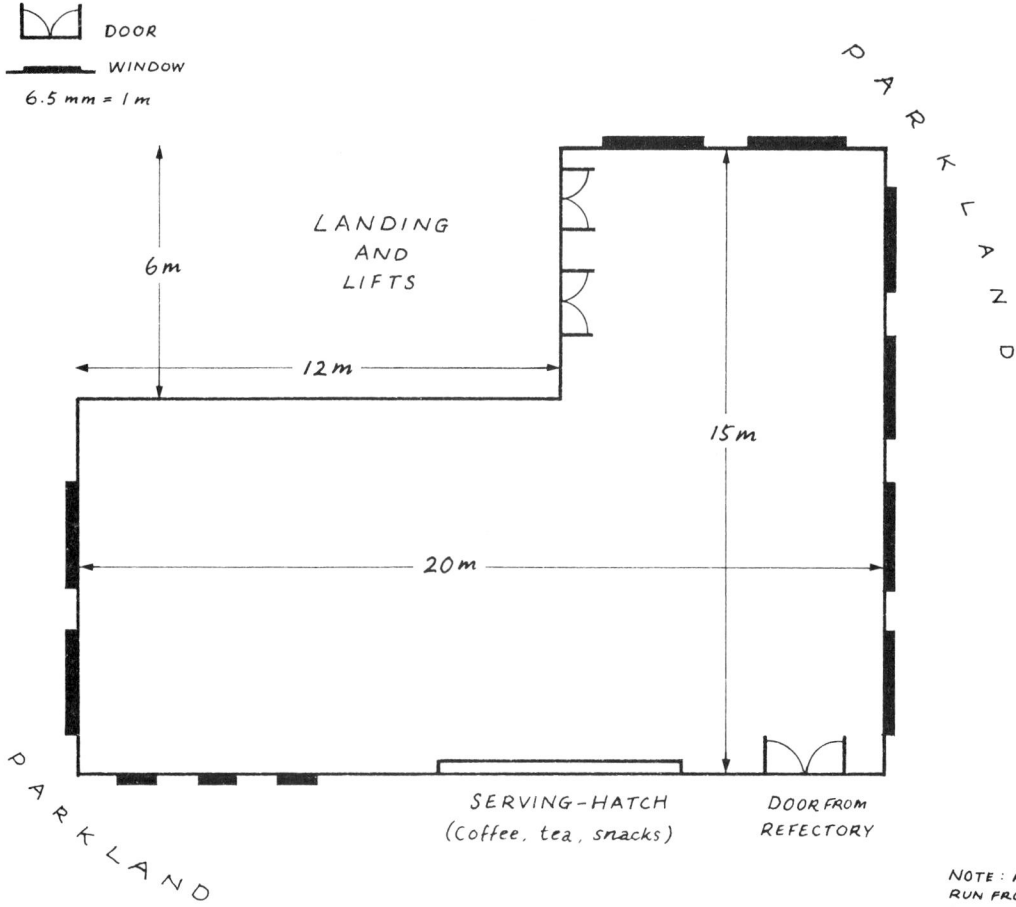

1. What area, in square metres, should be allocated to each of the activities and uses listed above?
2. Where should each area be situated in the Common Room?
3. Is the Common Room really big enough to accommodate satisfactorily all the activities? Has the Committee been too ambitious in its plans?

THE RIGHT WORDS IN THE RIGHT PLACE

Mrs Donovan, the Chief Librarian of the University, has just received a visit from a salesman. This person made some rather exaggerated claims for the photocopying machine he hopes the library will rent or buy. Now that the salesman has left, she is writing a memo to Dudley Morris, summarizing the information she was given about the machine.

You can read below what the salesman actually said. In the example, you can see how, in her memo, Mrs Donovan expresses the content of his remarks more factually and objectively. Complete the other sections of the memo in the same manner.

Example
> 'Of course, being a Japanese machine, it's ridiculously cheap. And don't forget, technically speaking, it makes the others look pretty silly. Our competitors will just have to go back to the drawing board, I'm afraid.'
>
> 'The salesman said that this Japanese-made machine was very cheap. He also claimed it was technically superior to other photocopiers on the market.'

1 'Take my word for it. The machine works like clockwork. You won't be calling our maintenance department every other day because you've got paper jammed in the works, or anything like that. And another thing, it's dead easy to reload with paper. You don't have to fiddle around with bits of machinery—just pop the sheets in the holder.'

2 'Look at this document I've just done. Fantastic, isn't it? You couldn't get a better copy than that now, could you? By the way, it'll do thirty a minute. Very fast, especially for such high-quality stuff.'

3 'You can buy or lease the machine. It's all the same to us. And you're welcome to try it out for a week or so, if you wish. Believe me, once you've used it, you won't want to know about any other. In our company, we don't go for high-pressure sales tactics; we let the product speak for itself.'

4 'Goodness me. One thing I forgot to mention. If you place an order with us before September, you'll get a fifteen per cent discount. We offer it only to educational institutions. Now, that's worth having, surely?'

WRITTEN ASSIGNMENT

> You are a member of a joint staff/student planning committee. You will not be able to attend the meeting at which the decision will be made concerning the chairs. Write a letter to Dudley Morris, apologizing for your absence and explaining which type or types of chair you would choose.

This letter need not be formal; it will begin *Dear Mr Morris* or *Dear Dudley*, and it will end *Yours sincerely* or perhaps simply *Yours*. For details of layout, see Appendix, Section 1.

APOLOGIZING
I regret that I cannot come to the meeting on . . .

I am sorry (to say) that I shall not be able to attend the meeting on . . .

This is because of a prior engagement/I have another appointment . . .

I have to/must take part in a conference/visit a research establishment . . . etc.

CHOOSING—AND EXPLAINING YOUR CHOICE
All/ Two / of the chairs that you describe look good value/very promising.

Only one/None of the chairs that you mention looks any good at all/really suitable.

From what you say, I should be inclined to buy 50 folding chairs and 100 of . . .

My choice/recommendation would be to . . .

I would recommend/suggest that . . .

Three of the chairs are obviously no use to us at all—namely/that is to say/i.e. . . . .

That leaves us only the . . . chair, which I would select as the best available/of a bad lot/for lack of anything better.

CONCLUDING YOUR LETTER
In a personal letter like this, avoid conventional or formal sentences at the end. If you feel your letter needs a short final sentence, make up one of your own—perhaps on these lines:
I hope the meeting goes well.
Anyway, good luck with the meeting.
I shall be very interested to hear what the committee finally chooses.

Additional assignment

On 1 March, a local department store delivers to you an elegant and expensive swivel chair—the latest model from a range of furniture specially manufactured for the store and bearing the store's brand name. As a university teacher, you naturally intended to use the chair as an easy chair in which you could relax and read the numerous books and articles necessary for your research and lectures. In the three months since you took delivery, you have had a number of problems with the chair.

These have included:
(a) failure of the swivel action
(b) collapse of the base due to failure of the rocking action of the chair—while you were sitting on it!
(c) deterioration of the chair cover
(d) loss of shape and firmness of the seat cushion
(e) tendency of stitches to come loose.

Write a strong letter of complaint to the manager of the store. Tell him that you wish to return the chair and get your money refunded.

HEARD IN THE COMMON ROOM

— What happened to that furniture store down by the station?
— They went broke years ago.

— They've got a nerve to ask £140 each for those chairs. Ridiculous!
— Yes, but surely you can beat them down, can't you?

— How many full-time students are there in this place?
— Off the cuff, I'd say about seven or eight thousand.

— My grant had better come soon. My bank manager is sending me rude letters.
— In the red again, are you?

— I see our Vice-Chancellor is appearing in yet another TV quiz show.
— Well, you know he likes the limelight.

— How on earth did Jackson become a Head of Department at twenty-nine?
— He was in the right place at the right time: that's all it boils down to.

— It's infuriating. The photocopier's broken down again—that's the third time this week.
— It's not worth calling the maintenance engineer. I think we should take it up with the management.

— I thought my maths was pretty good, but these equations are tricky.
— I know. I can't make head or tail of them.

— Er... Well—it's like this, you see. I was going to do the essay last night, but—
— All right, if you haven't done it, just say so! You needn't beat about the bush.

— Don't you think capitalism is dead?
— Um... Well, that's a bit of a loaded question...

1. Find out what these idioms mean.
2. How would you express these ideas without using an idiom?
3. Write your own dialogues including these idioms correctly and appropriately used.

UNDERSTANDING THE CASE

Read the case study in the Casebook and answer these questions.

1 In what sense is the Elite company a specialist shoe manufacturer?
2 To whom does the client record card belong?
3 What evidence is there that the Elite company plans to extend the range of its goods?
4 What exactly is the function of Marketing Personnel Services?
5 Why do companies use organizations like MPS?
6 What advantages do Elite hope to gain by appointing a Sales Representative instead of renewing their contract with the Far East Footwear Corporation?
7 What information given in Kazumichi's telephone call to Thompson suggests that MPS is an efficient organization?
8 Why does MPS collect information about the applicants' private lives?
9 How important do you consider academic qualifications to be for this post?
10 What kinds of previous experience, apart from selling footwear, might Elite be interested in, and why?

VOCABULARY Finding the right one

Nigel Thompson is talking about some of the problems of recruiting staff. Fill in the gaps in his remarks from the box below. There may be more than one possible choice. Not all the words in the box need be used. You may have to change the ending of a word, for example, to indicate the tense of a verb or to show that a noun is plural.

Thompson In making k_____ staff a_____ you've got to bear in mind a number of f_____. Obviously the a____'s b__ g__ is i_____. You're looking for good academic qu____, relevant e_____, and some evidence of the person's c_____ for success.

Attracting the right people is always difficult. That's why the _____ of personnel s_____ is often left to consultants who s_____ in such _____. An ambitious young man or woman wants something that offers wider s_____ for his _____, or more r_____. You've got to present the _____ as a c_____—something tough, but exciting.

But remember you also need specific personal qu_____ in the successful applicant: maybe a good h_____ for figures, or the k_____ of getting people to work in a team, or a f_____ for design. And the a_____ to get on well with other people—that's _____!

crucial	ability	experience
essential	background	qualification
important	capacity	record
key	flair	
	head	applicant
appointment	knack	selection
factor	talent	specialize
job		
quality	challenge	
task	responsibility	
work	scope	

MRS KATO IS INTERVIEWED BY THE BOARD

Read or listen to the dialogue.

As one of four short-listed applicants, Mrs Kato is called to Tokyo and interviewed by a board of two members: Mr Kazumichi and Mr Sheridan.

Kazumichi ... And now we're going to switch to English for a little while. I think Mr Sheridan has some questions he would like to ask.

Sheridan Thank you. Mrs Kato, my Japanese is not very good. I think I may have missed one or two points in what you were saying. For example, I notice you left school without taking the usual school-leaving examinations. How did that come about?

Kato Well ... actually, there were personal reasons why I couldn't finish my education. I'd rather not go into details. However, I have tried to make up for it since. I went to evening classes for five years; I have a certificate in book-keeping and a diploma in secretarial studies.

Sheridan Have you ever thought of going to university and taking a degree?

Kato Not really, no. It wouldn't be easy to get a place. I haven't got the minimum qualifications. But I understood this post didn't require a degree.

Sheridan You're quite right, of course. It doesn't. Frankly, we're more interested in your career background and your personal qualities. I see you've been promoted pretty rapidly in your present company. Forgive me for saying so, but that's unusual too, isn't it, in this country?

Kato Well, I suppose you could say that I'd have reached my present level much earlier if I'd been a university graduate. After all, I'm not really in a senior position, you know. That's why I'm looking for something bigger—more challenging.

Kazumichi What exactly does it involve, Mrs Kato—your present job, I mean?

Kato Oh, I purchase shoes from foreign suppliers mainly.

Kazumichi I'm sorry. Could you be a little more specific?

Kato Of course. I'm responsible for placing orders, chasing them up if they're delayed, allocating the annual budget for my department, negotiating with manufacturers, that sort of thing.

Sheridan Mrs Kato, could you give us some details now about the size of your department, how it's organized and so on.

1. Listen again and find as many expressions as possible which are used to get definite information or establish the facts.
2. Practise the expressions recorded after the dialogue on the tape.
3. With the following check-list to help you, do the role-playing exercise.

GETTING THE FACTS

I think I may have missed ...
What exactly ...?
Could you be a little more specific/precise?
Could you give us some details about ...?
Could you explain ...?
I'd like more information about ...
I'd like to hear more about ...
Anything else you can tell me about ...?
Tell me more about ...

Role-playing exercise

A key position at Elite (UK) has fallen vacant. Three short-listed candidates are to be interviewed in a conference room at a London hotel. The members of the interviewing team—all senior personnel at Elite—are going to question the candidates closely about three areas of their life and careers:
  (i) family background;
  (ii) educational history;
  (iii) work experience.
Where possible, students should use their own experience as a basis for the role-play.

WHY ARE THEY LEAVING?

The Managing Director of one of Elite's competitors is worried about labour turnover in the company—particularly in certain areas. He asks the Personnel Manager to send him the Termination of Employment Register for the last three-month period (January to March). He already has the figures for the number of employees in each department.

Study the tables below, and answer the questions as fully as you can.

1. How many people left each department in this three-month period?
2. What do the entries in the Register reveal about labour turnover in the five departments?
3. What kind of recommendations do you think the Personnel Manager might make to the Managing Director on how to improve the situation?

Table A

Distribution of Staff		Department Code in Table B
Production (full time)	100	P
Production (part time)	115	P
Field Sales	21	S
Transport	16	T
Design	8	D
Marketing	15	M
	275	

Table B

Register of Termination of Employment for Period Jan to Mar 1989					
DATE	NAME (MALES IN CAPITALS)	DEPT FT	DEPT PT	YEAR OF BIRTH	JOINED COMPANY	REASON FOR LEAVING
5.1	PATEL V.	P		1961	12.6.87	Discharged: caused accident
8.1	Kingsley K.A.		P	1944	2.8.88	Married
16.1	McLEOD J.	T		1956	18.3.83	Pressure from wife
25.1	HASKELL M.	P		1955	1.6.86	No reason given
28.1	Andrews S.		P	1972	4.1.89	Family moved North
28.1	Jacobson A.S.		P	1947	15.6.88	Baby
6.2	MULLIGAN P.	T		1961	1.6.87	To 'better himself'
14.2	HADJIFOTIOU E.	P		1969	27.3.87	Discharged: insubordinate
16.2	Singh S.	P		1969	21.4.88	No reason given
21.2	Daniels D.J.		P	1963	6.5.88	Dissatisfied
27.2	JESPERSEN C.	M		1924	3.10.64	Retired
5.3	Ogunlayo M.		P	1965	1.5.88	Could not adapt to work
8.3	HARDCASTLE J.	P		1929	3.8.64	Early retirement
17.3	ECKERSLEY S.J.	D		1957	10.1.83	To join industrial design Co.
26.3	GIOVANETTI C.	T		1970	8.2.86	Wanted better pay
30.3	O'Hara J.	P		1958	30.4.87	Wanted better pay
31.3	Blondel A.		P	1937	4.6.86	Bad health
31.3	LORD P.		P	1969	4.1.89	Constant rows with foreman

THE RIGHT WORDS IN THE RIGHT PLACE

Some time ago, Elite decided to create the post of Sales Director. To help them in their task, they used a specialist recruitment agency, Management Advisory Services Ltd, which is based in London.

> Below, two of the agency's executives are discussing what points they will include in the press advertisement for the post. The example shows how some of the information appears in the final advertisement. Complete the remaining paragraphs of the text.

Example

'OK then. Let's start by saying Elite's British and it makes shoes. Workforce? Over two hundred. And turnover, say £5 million or thereabouts. After that, we say they want a Sales Director for the UK and foreign markets. Right, so far, so good...'

SALES DIRECTOR   *Shoe industry*

Our client is a British shoe manufacturing company employing over 200 people and with a turnover of approximately £5 million per annum. They require a Sales Director to develop the company's business in the UK and overseas.

1. 'Let's see now, who would he or she report to? Mmm ... the General Manager. Yes, that's right. And the main job of this new Sales Director would be to boost the company's sales—here and overseas. Oh yes, this would be the right place to mention that advertising and market research will also come under the Sales Director's umbrella.'

2. 'Elite's not too worried about the age of the applicants. They'll consider anyone in the twenty-five to forty range. But they definitely want a graduate—someone with a degree in chemistry or mechanical engineering possibly. And they won't look at anyone who has less than two years' experience in sales—at managerial level, that is.'

3. 'They'd also like the person's experience to be in a technical field, but not necessarily in the shoe trade. We might as well mention here that someone with a qualification in shoe technology would be specially welcome, although it's obvious really.'

4. 'Now, salary. Not less than £18,000, that's for sure. The final figure will be agreed between Elite and the applicant. After the salary, we'll put in the bit about the perks—executive car, life assurance, pension plan, relocation expenses.'

5. 'We can end the ad by asking applicants to write or call you, Robert Sheridan—remind them everything will be confidential—and quote a reference number. Our address will be at the bottom, of course.'

WRITTEN ASSIGNMENT

> Write a letter applying for one of the vacancies advertised below. You should enclose a curriculum vitae and your letter should present the most important facts about your background and experience.

BIG OPPORTUNITIES

in

* **Marketing**
* **Research and Development**
* **Production**
* **Accounting**
* **Administration**

A major international company, about to establish a new manufacturing/retailing network in this country, seeks management expertise at all levels.

Competitive salaries, fringe benefits, good conditions of service and outstanding prospects for advancement will be offered to suitable candidates. Write in confidence, outlining your career so far, to Box 1234, *The Star*.

This letter should be brief and to the point. If the company are interested in you and want to know more about you, they will call you for interview.

HOW TO START

Say where you saw the advertisement.

> *With reference to your advertisement in* The Star *of 14 May...*
>
> *I saw your advertisement in* The Star, *dated May 14,...*
>
> *I refer to your advertisement in yesterday's* Star...

Then specify the type of job you are interested in.

> *I wish to be considered for a position on the marketing side...*
>
> *I am applying for a senior position in your Production Department...*
>
> *I hope you will consider me for a post in Research and Development...*

Next, give some facts about yourself: how old you are; your nationality; whether you are married or single; what level of education you have attained.

I am 34 years old, of Japanese nationality, and single. My education was interrupted, and for personal reasons, I was not able to finish secondary school.

I am Malaysian, aged 42, married, with two children. After completing my secondary education, I obtained a degree in Economics and a post-graduate diploma in Business Administration.

SAY WHAT YOU HAVE DONE—AND WHAT YOU ARE DOING

For the past five years, I have been working for a market research organization.

My previous work experience includes three years in sales with a manufacturer of household appliances, and two years as Brand Manager with a company selling food products.

I have ten years' experience in the management accounting field. At present, I am working as Company Secretary for . . .

CONCLUDING

Be very brief.

I hope to hear from you soon.

I can come for interview at any time which is convenient to you.

I shall be glad to send you any further particulars of my career that you may require.

I look forward to hearing from you soon.

Note: In this letter, and in all business documents, avoid using short forms of verbs. In other words, it is incorrect to write *don't*—write *do not*.

Additional assignment

As the Personnel Manager of Elite, write a memo to the Managing Director saying which of the four short-listed candidates you would select for the post of Far East Sales Representative, and why.

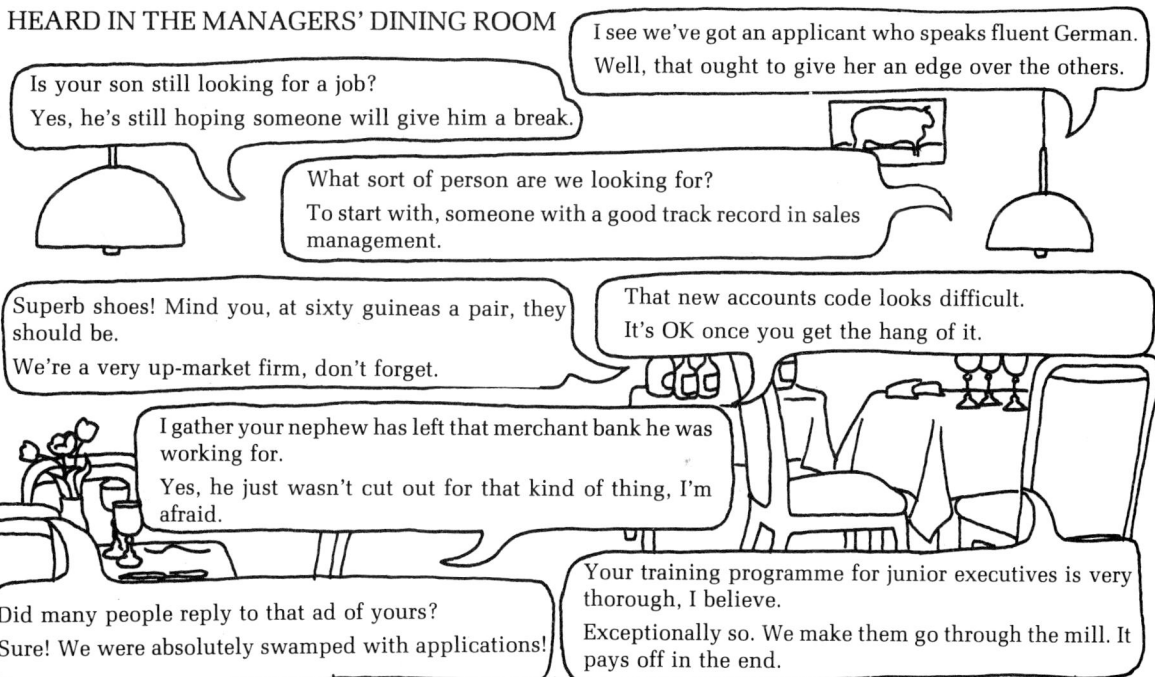

HEARD IN THE MANAGERS' DINING ROOM

Is your son still looking for a job?
Yes, he's still hoping someone will give him a break.

I see we've got an applicant who speaks fluent German. Well, that ought to give her an edge over the others.

What sort of person are we looking for?
To start with, someone with a good track record in sales management.

Superb shoes! Mind you, at sixty guineas a pair, they should be.
We're a very up-market firm, don't forget.

That new accounts code looks difficult.
It's OK once you get the hang of it.

I gather your nephew has left that merchant bank he was working for.
Yes, he just wasn't cut out for that kind of thing, I'm afraid.

Your training programme for junior executives is very thorough, I believe.
Exceptionally so. We make them go through the mill. It pays off in the end.

Did many people reply to that ad of yours?
Sure! We were absolutely swamped with applications!

Those orders still haven't been processed! Someone's slipped up.
I'm pretty sure I know who it is. I'm going to give Peter a rocket when he gets back from the pub.

1 Find out what these idioms mean.
2 How would you express these ideas without using an idiom?
3 Write your own dialogues including these idioms correctly and appropriately used.

FUNFABBRIX

UNDERSTANDING THE CASE

Read the case study in the Casebook and answer these questions.

1. What kind of person do you think the boss of Funfabbrix is?
2. What evidence is there that he wishes to keep the costs of running his business as low as possible?
3. What sort of relations exist between Benno Macari and the boss?
4. In what ways are safety regulations in this company being broken?
5. Why are safety regulations not being observed in this firm?
6. What caused Mrs Edna Whiteson to become specially concerned about the safety of the workers?
7. Although the workers do not belong to a trade union, their interests are not totally ignored. Explain this statement.
8. In what ways, if any, did the Fire Inspector's visit benefit the workers at Funfabbrix?
9. How does Mrs Whiteson show that she has a good sense of timing?
10. Why is Benno Macari now in a very difficult position?

VOCABULARY What's it like to work here?

Edna Whiteson expresses some frank opinions about her workplace. Fill in the gaps in her remarks from the box below. There may be more than one possible choice. Not all the words in the list need be used. You may have to change the ending of a verb or a noun.

Edna All my girls here are cl____ as machine o____, though the level of skill varies, I can tell you. The p____ and c____ can only be d____ as terrible. The b____ w____ for most of the girls is under £70 a week, which doesn't give you much of a l____ these days, although with o____ and b____ for piecework it generally amounts to £80 or £90. We're about due for another _____ soon; haven't had one for a year. Sweated labour, that's what it is. And this workshop c____ the Factories Act and the Health and Safety at Work Act and I don't know what else.

The fire regulations aren't properly o____, for a start. The Fire Certificate was only r____ this year on c____ that the boss i____ a sprinkler system. Sprinkler system! He won't even pay for us to have an electric kettle, the tight-fisted old so-and-so.

He says he can't _____ to r____ the fire escape; he can't _____ the money. I know what he's up to, the crafty devil. They're going to demolish this place and put up one of those big tower blocks. So the boss doesn't want to _____ anything on r____ the p____. He'd sooner we just quietly burned to death.

But we'll fix him. This overtime b____ will put young Benno right on the spot. It's our busiest time of year. Three days, and he'll lose his nerve. Then we've got him.

basic	bonus	class	instal
condition	overtime	classify	maintain
living		describe	renew
pay	afford		repair
rise	spare	contravene	
wage	spend	observe	ban
			operator
			premises

BLUNT WORDS FROM A FIRE INSPECTOR

Read or listen to the dialogue.
Mr McFadden, the local Fire Inspector, is talking to Benno Macari, Funfabbrix's Production Manager.

McFadden This won't do at all, Mr Macari. You know the fire regulations as well as I do.

Macari Do me a favour, Mr McFadden. If we obeyed all those fiddling regulations, we'd never get any work done . . .

McFadden Now look here. The regulations are for your safety. What's more, I can have this place closed down at a couple of hours' notice. You know that, don't you?

Macari OK. Anything you say.

McFadden Now: emergency exits. These must be kept clear at all times.

Macari I'll look into that right away.

McFadden Outside doors should be hooked open while the building is occupied. Inside doors should be shut—

Macari I'll see that they are, Mr McFadden.

McFadden That's not good enough. Inside doors must close automatically, but not lock.

Macari Yes, of course. You can rely on me to make sure that they do.

McFadden Good. Next point: you must ensure that there are no naked lights used in the workroom.

Macari But the girls have to brew up their tea! I can assure you, they're very careful.

McFadden Then they must have an electric kettle. That gas ring is a fire hazard.

Macari I'll do what I can.

McFadden Then there's the staircase. It needs three coats of fire-resistant paint.

Macari Rest assured, Mr McFadden: if those stairs get painted again, I'll see that they're fireproof.

McFadden And finally, the fire escape. I'd get a builder to give you an estimate. It's in urgent need of repair.

Macari I promise you—I'll give the matter top priority. You have my word that we'll observe the regulations to the letter.

1. Listen again and find as many expressions as possible which are used to promise action and reassure people that you are dealing with the problem.
2. Practise the expressions recorded after the dialogue on the tape.
3. With the following check-list to help you, do the role-playing exercise.

PROMISING ACTION

I'll look into . . . right away.
I'll see that . . .
I'll make sure that . . .
You can rely on me to . . .
I can assure you that . . .
Rest assured, I'll . . .
I promise you, I'll . . .
You have my word, I'll . . .
I'll see to . . .
I'll do what I can.

Role-playing exercise

Macari's boss is not happy. The local Health and Safety Inspector has finally tracked him down and summoned him to appear at his office. The boss takes Benno Macari with him—for moral support and to play the role of scapegoat, if necessary. The Inspector and his assistant have plenty of ammunition to fire at Funfabbrix:
  (i) the workers do not wear protective clothing;
  (ii) safety guards are removed;
  (iii) no safety committee has been set up;
  (iv) bad sanitation and washing facilities;
  (v) grease on the floor;
  (vi) dangerous fire escape, etc. etc. . . .

STAYING OUT OF TROUBLE

A lot of the machines in the Funfabbrix workshop are out of date and falling to pieces. Macari estimates that their inefficiency is costing the firm at least £10,000 a year in lost production. The boss, however, is very unwilling to put money into new equipment, even when Macari shows him his costings for replacement and reconditioning. The figures are as follows:

Items of equipment	Replacement (unit cost) £	Reconditioning (unit cost) £
20 sewing machines	260	40
2 multiple pattern cutters	895	120
2 auto steam pressers	1,325	350

New machines should give at least five years' service without major repairs. The existing machines, even if reconditioned, cannot be relied on for more than 12 months. Machinery prices are rising at the moment by an average of about 20 per cent a year.

Examine the figures and answer these questions. As far as possible, do all the calculations in your head, and speak the figures aloud while you calculate. The answers don't have to be exact; estimates will do, but you should try to reach them quickly and reasonably accurately.

1. Macari is pretty sure he can get at least 5 per cent discount on bulk orders for new equipment. Roughly how much would it cost him to replace all the items shown above?

2. If he has the existing machines reconditioned, and then has to replace them in a year or so, how much will this cost altogether?

3. The boss is eventually convinced by Macari's argument, and agrees to spend £6,000. It is, after all, tax-deductible, and the real cost to him will be negligible. How can Macari best allocate this money?

THE RIGHT WORDS IN THE RIGHT PLACE

Just before Mr McFadden, the Fire Inspector, leaves Funfabbrix Fashions, he has a final word with Benno Macari.

McFadden I'm glad you realize the seriousness of the situation, Mr Macari. Let me remind you once again of what we agreed. You've promised for your part, that none of your girls will be allowed to light up in *No Smoking* areas in the building. I don't need to tell you again how important that particular regulation is. You've also given your word that all the fire extinguishers will be checked. If you find any which are not up to scratch, you'll replace them. There'll be no more brewing of tea on the gas ring, and the boxes in front of the fire exit will be gone by tomorrow. We've discussed the problem of the fire escape. OK, I accept you won't be able to get a new one put in right away; but don't forget, you'll call in a contractor to give you an estimate of the cost of replacing that rusty contraption. Once I know this, I can have a chat with your boss and find out when the work might be done. One final thing—I'm trusting you to keep your part of the bargain. I'm going to send you a schedule of work to be done within the next two months to make this place safe. Now you mark my words, if you don't get moving on this pretty quickly, you and your company will be in very hot water indeed.

> When he gets back to his office, Mr McFadden begins to draft a letter which he will send to Macari. In it, he will summarize and confirm in writing the remarks he made to the Production Manager as he was leaving Funfabbrix's premises. As you can see, the Fire Inspector has already written a few lines of this letter. It is your task to complete it. Insert a suitable letter heading.

Dear Mr Macari
During a recent inspection of your company's premises, I discovered numerous breaches of the fire and safety regulations. I now confirm in writing the points we agreed during our discussion of this serious matter . . .

WRITTEN ASSIGNMENT

> Benno Macari has decided to put a notice on the board near the entrance to the workshop. He will appeal to all staff to cooperate in observing the fire and safety regulations; in particular, he will stress the importance of complying with *No Smoking* signs. Write the notice for him.

This type of communication must be clear, and convey the right tone. Macari will want to sound firm, but will avoid giving the impression of being dictatorial. Don't forget, he is already having difficulty maintaining good relations with his staff.

In the text of the message, you should mention:

(i) the Fire Inspector's visit;
(ii) the fact that fire and safety regulations are being constantly disobeyed;
(iii) the need to observe these regulations—especially the *No Smoking* notices;
(iv) the possibility the fire certificate will not be re-issued—unless improvements are made.

The following points are worth bearing in mind:

* Be very selective when deciding what to put in the text of the notice. People will not bother to read a long wordy message.

* Avoid complicated language. Write simply and directly. Use short sentences—or phrases. A single word, in capitals or bold type, can be highly effective.

* Start with an eye-catching headline or opening sentence—if you wish. After all, you are trying to attract people's attention. You may choose some device or display technique to achieve this aim, for example, by using a felt-tipped pen to write the notice or by printing the heading in a different colour from the text itself.

Make sure you sign the notice.

Alternative assignment

Imagine you are either Benno Macari, Mrs Whiteson or one of the female workers at Funfabbrix. Write a letter to a friend living outside Britain complaining about working conditions in the firm. Describe one or two of the important personalities among the staff, and give some details about the present crisis, following the Fire Inspector's visit. You may, if you wish, mention how the problem has been—or will be—resolved.

HEARD AT THE TOP OF THE STAIRS

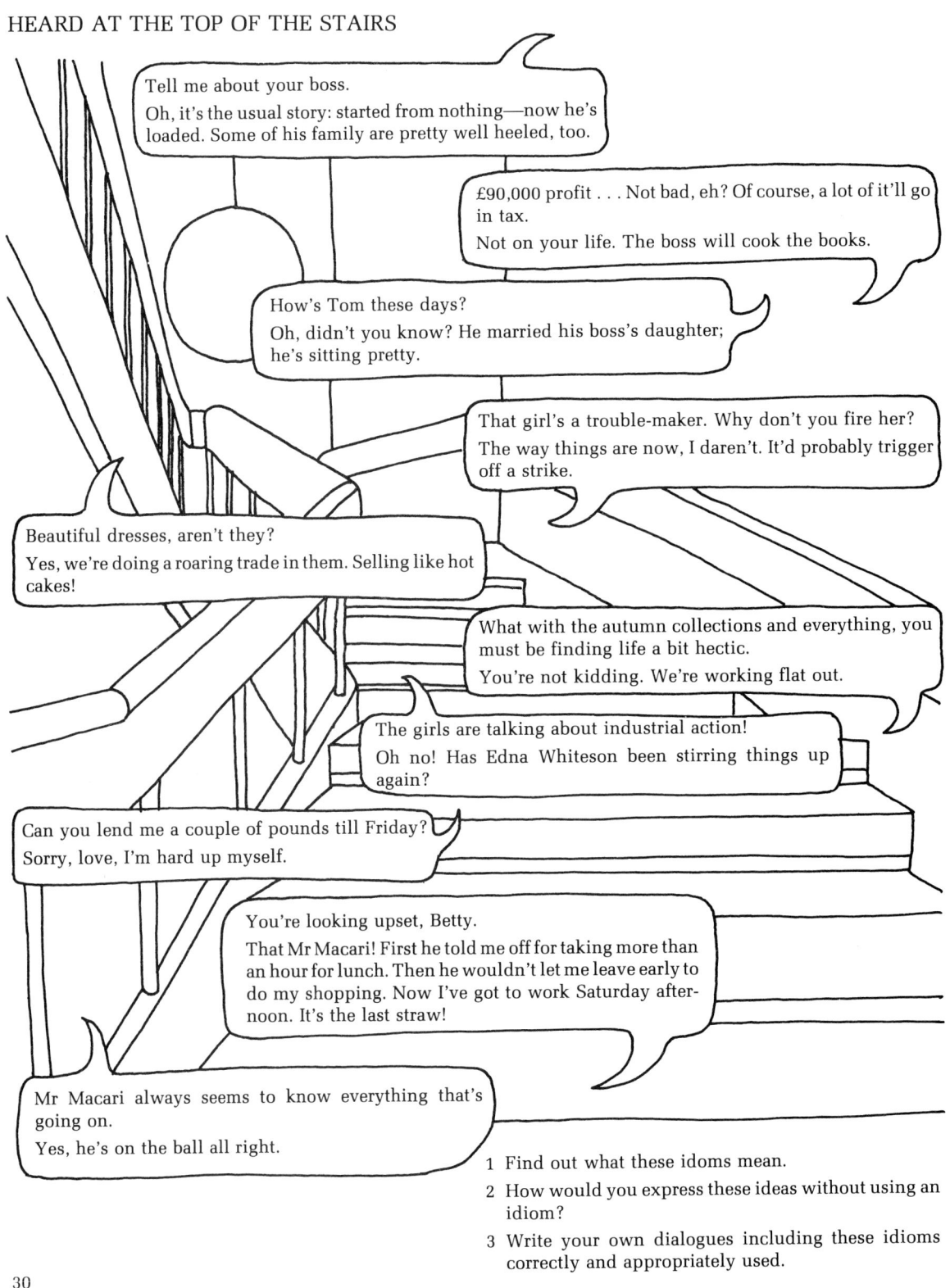

- Tell me about your boss.
- Oh, it's the usual story: started from nothing—now he's loaded. Some of his family are pretty well heeled, too.

- £90,000 profit... Not bad, eh? Of course, a lot of it'll go in tax.
- Not on your life. The boss will cook the books.

- How's Tom these days?
- Oh, didn't you know? He married his boss's daughter; he's sitting pretty.

- That girl's a trouble-maker. Why don't you fire her?
- The way things are now, I daren't. It'd probably trigger off a strike.

- Beautiful dresses, aren't they?
- Yes, we're doing a roaring trade in them. Selling like hot cakes!

- What with the autumn collections and everything, you must be finding life a bit hectic.
- You're not kidding. We're working flat out.

- The girls are talking about industrial action!
- Oh no! Has Edna Whiteson been stirring things up again?

- Can you lend me a couple of pounds till Friday?
- Sorry, love, I'm hard up myself.

- You're looking upset, Betty.
- That Mr Macari! First he told me off for taking more than an hour for lunch. Then he wouldn't let me leave early to do my shopping. Now I've got to work Saturday afternoon. It's the last straw!

- Mr Macari always seems to know everything that's going on.
- Yes, he's on the ball all right.

1. Find out what these idoms mean.
2. How would you express these ideas without using an idiom?
3. Write your own dialogues including these idioms correctly and appropriately used.

UNDERSTANDING THE CASE

Read the case study in the Casebook and answer these questions.

1 Which is the chief selling point of the electronic fencer manufactured by JCS?
2 What do you think could be some of the problems associated with marketing this type of product?
3 Specify some of the technical advantages possessed by the JCS fencer which make it superior to other models.
4 Why are the Canadian orders important to John Connell?
5 Why does Joe Maskie now find himself 'over a barrel'?
6 How can one explain Joe Maskie's uncompromising attitude towards John Connell concerning the fencers?
7 Why are the sales figures for 1988 disappointing?
8 What is most noteworthy about the Belgium/Holland market?
9 Why could the Joachim Carpels organization be particularly useful to JCS?
10 Is it fair to say that John Connell showed poor judgement when he signed the contract with Joe Maskie in November?

VOCABULARY Selling overseas

In a hotel in Frankfurt, John Connell of JCS meets Dieter Proll, Sales Director of a firm that manufactures household goods. They exchange information about their distribution methods and problems. Fill in the gaps in their remarks in the usual way.

Connell In Europe we m_____ our g_____ through d_____. They buy on their own a____t and hold st____ in their own w__ h__. They also provide a____-s____ s____. What about your company? How do you set about it?

Proll Well, Switzerland is our biggest market and we've set up our own sales s_____ there. In Greece we have just one man, a very efficient s_____ r_____ who's been with us for more than ten years. Elsewhere, we use a____. We give them _____ r_____ to sell our goods in their area, and we pay them generous commissions. We sometimes go as high as fifteen per cent as an extra _____ to an agent if we're about to l_____ a new p____.

Connell You've obviously got a bigger d_____ n w_____ than we have. But you were telling me earlier that you've got a large number of o_____, but not sufficient p_____ c_____ to keep up with the orders!

Proll That's correct, up to a point. We can't s_____ new markets at present. So we're allowing reputable manufacturers to produce our goods under l_____. We're also looking at j_____-v_____ projects. We'll supply the technical expertise, and our partner will contribute manufacturing f_____ and a marketing s_____-u_____.

capacity	account	exclusive
facility	after-sales	incentive
network	distribution	licence
outlet	distributor	rights
set-up	launch	
warehouse	market	agent
	service	joint-venture
goods		representative
product		subsidiary
production		
sale		
stock		

31

OPPORTUNITY IN SOUTH AMERICA?

Read or listen to the dialogue.

At an agricultural fair John Connell meets a wealthy Colombian businessman, Senor Louis Rivero. The two men arrange to have dinner together at John's hotel.

Rivero Tell me, Mr Connell, have you ever thought of exporting to South America? Your electric fencer could do very well in our part of the world. So could your electric gate, for that matter.

Connell Quite honestly, we haven't made any attempt to penetrate the South American market. As I said, we're not really a big outfit. We don't have the financial resources to mount a large-scale exporting operation. In any case, our production capacity is limited. We're at full stretch at the moment.

Rivero Really? Well, you must be looking for bigger premises then, or are you planning to expand your present factory?

Connell Well, I'm not sure I want to get much bigger. I can handle things very well now. If we begin to expand . . .

Rivero I understand. More headaches, managerial problems, more pressure, a bigger slice to the taxman.

Connell Exactly.

Rivero You mentioned earlier you had an agent in Belgium and Holland. Have you considered using any other method of developing overseas sales?

Connell What do you mean? Our own subsidiary? An export salesman on the spot? Using an export house?

Rivero No, I was thinking of licensing agreements.

Connell I see. Well, up to now we've never been involved in that type of arrangement.

Rivero It's often worth doing, especially if you have capacity problems. My company has agreements with several European firms. Usually, we get manufacturing and sales rights, and of course, we pay royalties based either on turnover figures or on output.

Connell Hmm, that's very interesting.

Rivero How would you feel about my company manufacturing your fencer under licence? We have plenty of skilled labour and a very efficient sales force. We've also got some excess capacity . . .

Connell I really don't know. This would be something completely new for us. I'll have to think this one over carefully.

1 Listen again and find as many expressions as possible which are used to test how someone might react to a proposal you intend to make.

2 Practise the expressions recorded after the dialogue on the tape.

3 With the following check-list to help you, do the role-playing exercise.

SOUNDING SOMEONE OUT

Tell me, have you ever thought of . . .?
You must be ——ing . . .
Have you ever considered ——ing . . .?
I was thinking you might be interested in ——ing . . .
How would you feel about . . .?
I wonder if you've ever considered the possibility of . . .?
By the way, do you have much experience of . . .?
You know, it might be a good idea to . . .
We might well be interested in ——ing . . .

Role-playing exercise

Paul Hawkins works as a salesman for a firm of agricultural machinery manufacturers based in London. He gets a good basic salary of £12,000 per annum; he also receives a commission on sales, and has the use of a company car. Since he covers the southwest of England, John Connell and the Sales Manager both know him fairly well, and are aware he is a dynamic and talented salesman. One day, they meet Paul and invite him to come over to the factory. While having coffee in the canteen, the two men will use this opportunity to find out if Paul would consider joining JCS. They are, of course, prepared to offer him certain inducements.

DOWN ON THE FARM

Mr Giles of Sunnybrook Farm is one of JCS's oldest customers. On this page you can see a view of part of the farm, with the farmhouse surrounded by fields. Giles has grown crops in these fields for the last few years, but this year he is going to put cows into them. Unfortunately, the hedges and fences have fallen into disrepair, and Giles has only 1,000 metres of wire and two *Livewire* units with which to keep the cows in.

Consider the problem, and advise Giles how he should run his wire in order to enclose the largest possible area for his cows. Measurements are in metres. The wire does not have to form a closed loop in order to conduct current. The farmhouse and buildings are enclosed by a brick wall with strong gates. The wire cannot cross gateways or farm roads.

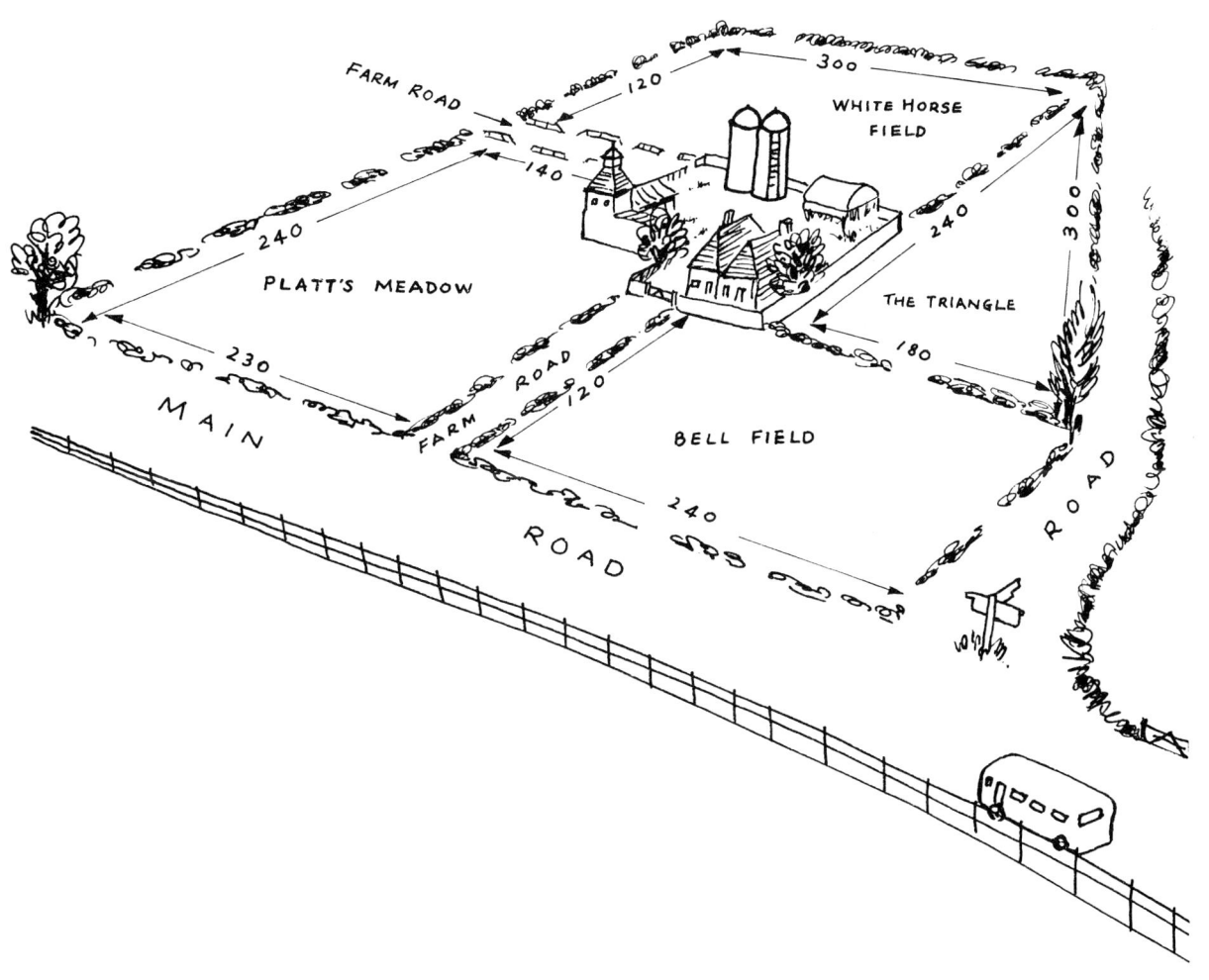

THE RIGHT WORDS IN THE RIGHT PLACE

The telex reproduced below has been sent by Joachim Carpels, JCS's agent in the Netherlands. John Connell is now going over to the factory to discuss its contents with his Production Manager, Jack Dawson. Using information given in the telex, write the dialogue which will take place between the two men.

Connell Hello, Jack. Could I have a word with you a minute. I've just received this telex from Joachim.

Dawson Oh good. What news from him?

Connell. . .

```
38210 JCS POOLE DORSET

62510 CARPELS BRUSSELS

ATTENTION CONNELL

URGENTLY REQUIRE 6 UNITS PLUS 12,000 METRES FENC-
ING. 2 UNITS MUST BE SUITABLE FOR ATTACHMENT TO
GATEPOST OR WALL. INCLUDE INSTRUCTION BOOKLETS.
SEND CONSIGNMENT BY AIR FREIGHT C/O OUR FORWARD-
ING AGENTS TO EINDHOVEN. NEW CUSTOMER. BIGGEST
LANDOWNER IN NETHERLANDS. EAGER TO MEET YOU
PERSONALLY. BIG POTENTIAL. REGARDING 100
RECHARGEABLE LAMPS ORDERED DECEMBER 28. WHERE
ON EARTH ARE THEY? CUSTOMER BREATHING DOWN MY
NECK. PLEASE CHECK SOONEST WITH JACK. HOPE HE IS
FEELING BETTER. GIVE HIM MY REGARDS.

JOACHIM CARPELS
```

WRITTEN ASSIGNMENT

Imagine that you have just joined JCS as Safety Officer. This is a new appointment, created to reduce the possibility of industrial accidents. One of your first tasks is to make sure that, if an accident does occur, the details are immediately put on record. This may help to identify potential hazards.

> Devise a simple but comprehensive Accident Report Form. It should elicit all the information that the Safety Officer needs, but it must not be too complex or contain a lot of unnecessary questions.

TACKLING THE PROBLEM

Don't try to make the form deal with every imaginable accident. You may prefer to limit it to certain types of accident—for example, those involving personal injury.

* Who is to complete the form after an accident? (Different sections may be filled in by different people.) Brief instructions for completing the form may have to be included.

Remember the purpose of the form: to help reduce accidents. The management are looking for a pattern of events; a particular employee, a particular machine, a certain time of day or week or year, may be especially associated with accidents.

* What information must the form ask for in every case?

Every accident is unique; therefore, you cannot devise a set of detailed questions about what happened. Parts of the form will be left blank, and the person who completes it will describe the event in his own words.

* What help can the form give to someone who is trying to describe what happened?

Finally, give instructions about who the form is to be sent to when it has been completed.

> Just as your form is being approved, you yourself have an accident. Your foot slips in a patch of oil on the factory floor—you land heavily, breaking your left arm and knocking over a stack of fragile components, most of which are smashed. After hospital treatment, your first task is to fill in an Accident Report Form—all the relevant sections of it.

Alternative assignment

In the dialogue, a Colombian businessman, Luis Rivero, sounds out John Connell about the possibility of manufacturing the *Livewire* fencer under licence. Senor Rivero is now staying at a hotel in Mayfair, London W1. Imagine that you are John Connell, and write a letter to Rivero, letting him know whether you accept or reject his proposal. Whatever you have decided, remember that Luis Rivero is an influential businessman who could be useful to your company in the future.

HEARD OUTSIDE THE SALES MANAGER'S OFFICE

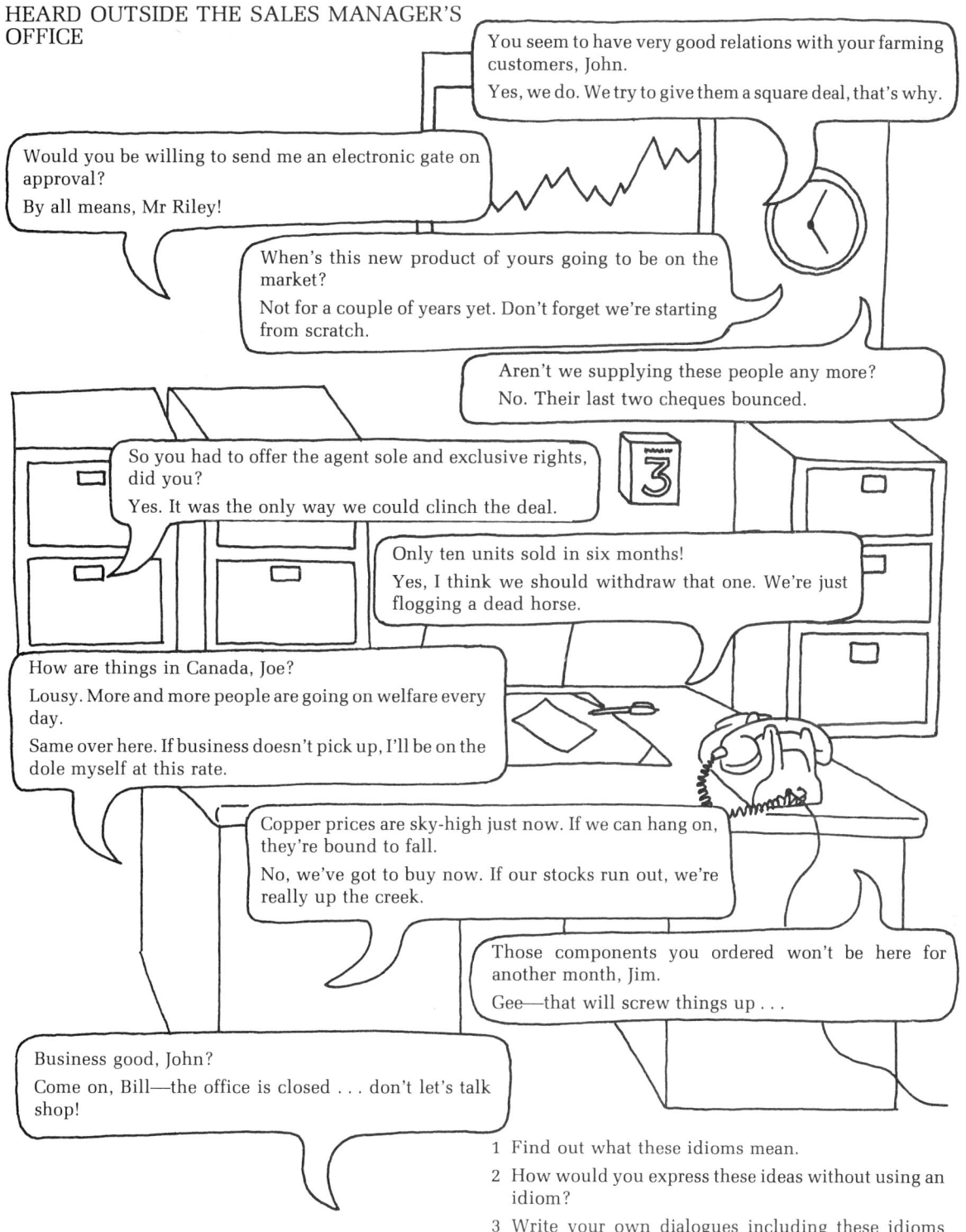

— You seem to have very good relations with your farming customers, John.
— Yes, we do. We try to give them a square deal, that's why.

— Would you be willing to send me an electronic gate on approval?
— By all means, Mr Riley!

— When's this new product of yours going to be on the market?
— Not for a couple of years yet. Don't forget we're starting from scratch.

— Aren't we supplying these people any more?
— No. Their last two cheques bounced.

— So you had to offer the agent sole and exclusive rights, did you?
— Yes. It was the only way we could clinch the deal.

— Only ten units sold in six months!
— Yes, I think we should withdraw that one. We're just flogging a dead horse.

— How are things in Canada, Joe?
— Lousy. More and more people are going on welfare every day.
— Same over here. If business doesn't pick up, I'll be on the dole myself at this rate.

— Copper prices are sky-high just now. If we can hang on, they're bound to fall.
— No, we've got to buy now. If our stocks run out, we're really up the creek.

— Those components you ordered won't be here for another month, Jim.
— Gee—that will screw things up . . .

— Business good, John?
— Come on, Bill—the office is closed . . . don't let's talk shop!

1. Find out what these idioms mean.
2. How would you express these ideas without using an idiom?
3. Write your own dialogues including these idioms correctly and appropriately used.

WATCHMERE

UNDERSTANDING THE CASE
Read the case study in the Casebook and answer these questions.

1. How big is Watchmere hospital?
2. In what sense has the hospital's development been unplanned?
3. For what reasons do you think the Medical Records Department became known as 'the hut'?
4. Who works in the Medical Records Department?
5. What part of their work do the medical secretaries probably enjoy most?
6. What mistake, if any, did Mrs Holmes make when dealing with the workers involved in the heating incident?
7. Is it fair to call the staff involved in that incident 'rebel workers'?
8. Why does the Group Secretary suggest in a memo to the Hospital Secretary that the matter 'needs to be handled delicately'?
9. For what purpose does the Group Secretary wish to see Mrs Holmes's work record?
10. Which of the pieces of evidence, if any, show Mrs Holmes in a bad light?

VOCABULARY What can we save money on?

Jim Devenish, the Hospital Secretary, discusses the difficulties he faces as a result of shortage of money. Fill in the gaps in his remarks in the usual way.

Devenish As you know, our budget has been cut again, and we are being called on to make _____ throughout the hospital s_____. One way we could achieve this _____ would be to p_____ o_____ some of our agency nurses and other staff who work on a part-time _____. These people do very valuable work, but they are not in_____.

If we start getting rid of full-time staff, then we must expect strong opposition from the unions involved. Our first _____ must be to maintain good labour r_____. You can't run a hospital without the g_____ w_____ and c_____ of the people who work in it, and it's certainly not my _____ to try.

In present _____ c conditions, there's bound to be strong c_____ for the limited r_____ that are available. Last year we put in c_____ for thirty extra administrative staff, but the General Management Committee r_____ every single one, or very nearly. I think the only c_____ we got out of them was the appointment of three temporary clerks in Medical Records.

I sometimes wonder if we couldn't d_____ with all this record-keeping altogether. Or put all the records into a computer; that'd be much more _____ al. But of course the lack of _____ s would r_____ o_____ the purchase of the computer to start with.

basis	concession	competition
service	cut	cooperation
system	economic	goodwill
	economical	relations
aim	economy	
goal		claim
intention	dispense	funds
objective	eliminate	indispensable
target	phase out	lack
	reject	request
	rule out	resources

A LOSING BATTLE

Read or listen to the dialogue.
Some of Watchmere's buildings are in very poor condition. A committee is now meeting to discuss the maintenance problems of the hospital.

Dr Frederick *(Chairman of the medical staff)* Something's got to be done. The place is going to fall to bits soon. How can I maintain the reputation of the unit in these conditions? I can't accept patients who desperately need treatment, and I'm discharging others before they really ought to go.

Jim *(Hospital Secretary)* It's obvious we can't go on any longer like this. I've got people working round the clock to repair that ceiling. It's lucky some of the other wards were empty because of the staff shortage. At least we were able to transfer patients to them. I don't know what we would have done otherwise.

Dr Frederick We must also have the gas and electricity supply pipes checked right away. I hear we have trouble in the Records Department because of lack of heating.

Jim Don't remind me, for goodness' sake!

Barbara *(Wife of local MP)* Let's face it, we're really fighting a losing battle here. We need at least one million—maybe two million—pounds just to maintain the hospital in a reasonable condition.

Jim You're absolutely right, Barbara, but I don't see how we're going to get it. We're way over budget, and there's no end in sight.

Dr Frederick Can't you get your husband to try to raise the matter in Parliament, Barbara? Lobby other MPs, that sort of thing. After all, the Orthopaedic Unit takes patients from all over the country, so surely the hospital would qualify for a special grant.

Barbara I'll do my best, Freddy. Honestly, this situation is a disgrace. I don't think even Florence Nightingale would have wanted to work here.

1. Listen again and find as many expressions as possible which are used to persuade people that a crisis has been reached, and that urgent action is now required.
2. Practise the expressions recorded after the dialogue on the tape.
3. With the following check-list to help you, do the role-playing exercise.

CREATING A SENSE OF URGENCY

Something's got to be done.

It's obvious that we can't go on any longer like this.

We must have this done right away.

This is a very urgent matter indeed.

Honestly, this situation is a disgrace.

We've got to do something right away.

It's time we did something about . . .

It's essential that we get someone to . . .

The first thing we've got to do is to . . .

Our first priority is to . . .

Role-playing exercise

In the last month, on three occasions, a quantity of ampoules and tablets have been removed illegally from the Dangerous Drugs cupboard in Medical Ward A. The day and night sisters in charge of the ward have arranged a meeting with Jim Devenish (Hospital Secretary) and David Miller (Group Secretary). They want the administration to take urgent action to stop the thefts. Both Devenish and Miller are aware of the seriousness of the situation, but do not want too much publicity to be given to the matter since drugs such as heroin and morphine have been removed. At present, the procedure for getting drugs is as follows: two nurses must go to the cupboard and sign a book, in which they note down the date and the quantity of drugs taken. There are six day nurses and two night nurses who have access to the cupboard.

TIME OUT

You are the head of one section of the Medical Records Department at Watchmere. This is the Statistical Section, always known as MR/Stats. There are 12 people in the section, and each is entitled to 20 days' paid leave a year, plus public holidays. The Leave Chart hangs on the wall of your office. Part of it is shown below. Today is the last day of June, and the holiday season is approaching. You need at least 8 people in the section, preferably 10, if you are to keep up with the work.

Study the chart and then consider how you might cope with each of the crises that are listed below.

Note: This chart does not show weekends. 30 August is a Bank Holiday.

Binns, Bray, Golan and Hall all have school-age children. School holidays are from 26 July to 6 September.

Mrs Bray has an appointment with a heart specialist in London on 8 July. Mr Jones is going on a training course in office efficiency from 9 to 11 August.

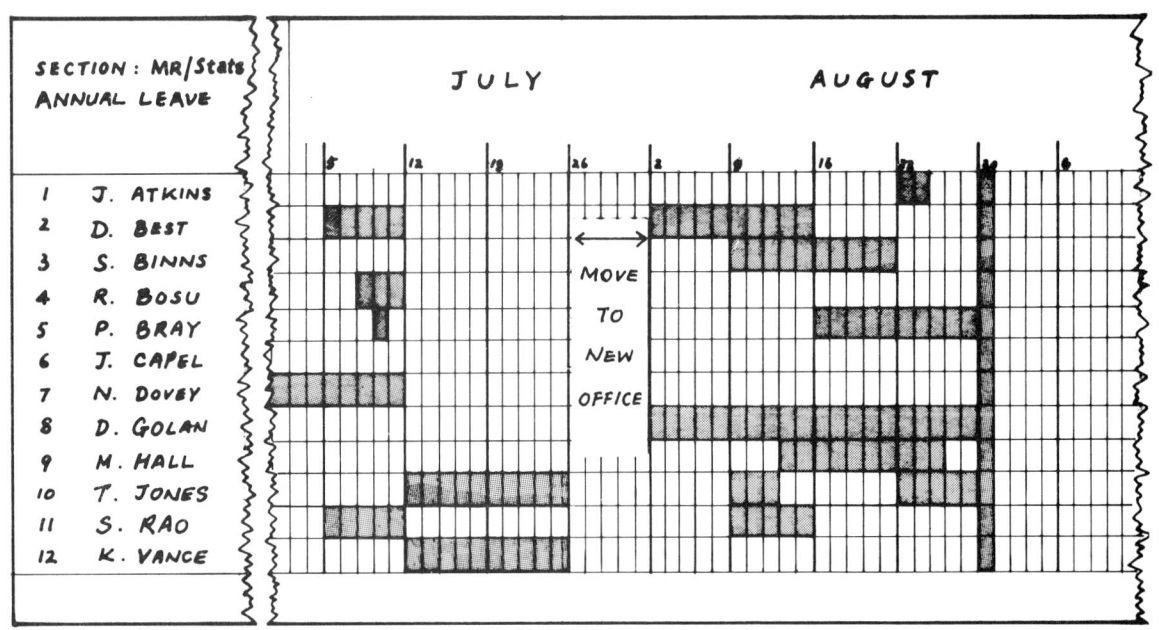

1. Miss Capel asks you for 14 days' leave, preferably in August. Can you fit this in?
2. Group ring up to say that a VIP from the Department of Health is coming to Watchmere on 8 July and wants to see the work of the Section. This means that you must have at least 9 people on duty. How are you going to manage this?
3. The Estates Committee has just decided to put back the move to MR/Stats' new office by a fortnight. You have carefully kept the week of 26 July free of leave commitments because you must have a full staff during the move. What are you to do?
4. Group tell you you can spend up to £400 a month on temporary secretarial assistance. A temp costs about £30 a day. What use will you make of this facility?

THE RIGHT WORDS IN THE RIGHT PLACE

After meeting Miss Patel, Jim Devenish called Mrs Holmes and asked her to come to his office to discuss the heating incident. As you will see his talk with her was far from pleasant.

> Below, you are given part of a telephone conversation between Jim Devenish and David Miller. Devenish is telling the Group Secretary about his meeting with Mrs Holmes. Miller requests him to send a memo, setting down in writing the essential points he is now making. Using only the information given in the dialogue, draft the text of the memo Devenish will send to Miller.

Devenish Honestly, David, I was very careful about what I said to her. Everyone knows you've got to handle Sheila with kid gloves. But you know, the very moment I suggested she'd been a little lax in dealing with those workers . . .

Miller Ah, maybe you shouldn't have put it that way, Jim. Let's not forget that she was in a very tricky situation.

Devenish Look, I know that. But, still, she reacted so . . . er . . . irrationally . . . yes, that's the right word, when I made that point. She started accusing me of constantly undermining her authority. Said I was always picking on her. Oh yes, and that I didn't appreciate what a strain she was under, trying to run the Records Section efficiently. Now, I ask you, how can you solve problems when someone has that kind of attitude?

Miller Mmm . . . Well, anyway, how does she suggest we deal with the present crisis?

Devenish Can't you guess? She wants us to ignore the incident. She feels she did the right thing in the circumstances and doesn't want to discuss it any further. Now doesn't that just prove how incompetent she is? No understanding of her staff. No willingness to compromise. I'm telling you, David, that woman's got to go. She's just not cut out to be a departmental head.

Miller I'd rather not comment on that at the moment, Jim, if you don't mind. Tell me, how are we going to calm things down in Sheila's department?

Devenish Quite frankly, David, I think the time's come for you to step in and deal with the matter. I'm not trying to pass the buck; it's just that everyone concerned would listen to you, and respect your judgement.

CONFIDENTIAL
To: Group Secretary   From: Hospital Secretary
Subject: Conversation with Mrs Holmes in connection with work stoppage in Medical Records Department

WRITTEN ASSIGNMENT

> Imagine you are David Miller, Group Secretary. The newly appointed Director of Personnel has asked you to write a special report, assessing Mrs Holmes's performance as Head of the Medical Records Department, and making a recommendation as to whether she should remain in her present position. Using information given in the case study, and adding any other facts you think necessary, write the report that is required. (For notes on report writing, see Appendix, section 4.)

ASSEMBLING THE FACTS

Mostly, David Miller will use the information given in the case study. However, having checked through Mrs Holmes's personal file, he will have this additional data:

(a) Mrs Holmes joined the department as a medical secretary five years ago. A year later, she was made its head. Previous to joining the hospital, she ran a nurses' employment agency which went bankrupt.

(b) In a recent report on her performance, Jim Devenish wrote that she seemed 'to have difficulties maintaining harmonious relations in her department'. Mrs Holmes, refusing to sign the report, had appended this note: 'Because of the mixed composition of the department, it is inevitable there will be minor disagreements among staff.'

(c) There have been no outside criticisms of the department's efficiency.

PRESENTING THE INFORMATION

Use the customary format to present your material.

(a) *Title*: Report on Mrs S. Holmes, Head of . . .

(b) *Terms of reference*: remember that the Director of Personnel asked you for the report: *On the instructions of . . . to assess the performance of . . . and to make a recommendation . . .*

(c) *Procedure*: you have examined Mrs Holmes's personal file, you have received a report from Mr Devenish, and you have talked to him about the matter. You also have your own knowledge and experience to draw upon.

(d) *Findings*: give a balanced assessment of Mrs Holmes's work record. Present the positive and negative aspects of her performance. If you give someone else's opinion of her capabilities, make it clear to the reader that it is an opinion—not a fact.

(e) *Conclusions*: here, you will analyse and interpret the facts you have presented:

> *There is evidence that . . .*
> *It would appear that . . .*
> *It seems obvious that . . .*
> *The conclusion one must draw is that . . .*

(f) *Recommendations*: this section will probably be quite short. *In view of the facts presented above, I recommend that . . .* You might then sum up your arguments very briefly.

Finally, date the report, and sign it.

Alternative assignment

Jim Devenish has decided to write a memo to all the clerical workers involved in the heating incident, informing them of the action he has decided to take in this matter. He will obviously be as diplomatic as possible—he does not want a minor disturbance to become a major dispute—but he will make it clear that, in future, the hospital authorities will deal severely with any employee who fails to carry out his or her duties. Draft this memo for Devenish.

HEARD IN THE REST ROOM

- Some drugs have disappeared from the Poison Cupboard.
- Oh boy! Someone's going to be on the carpet for that.

- Is it true there's trouble in Medical Records?
- Oh, the heating broke down or something. They're all up in arms.

- That new anaesthetist likes the sound of his own voice.
- You're telling me. Can't get a word in edgeways when he's around.

- Sheila and Jim don't seem to hit it off, do they?
- Well, it's high time they settled their differences, if you ask me.

- How do you rate David Miller as Group Secretary?
- Very highly. He's a very sound administrator, and he's not afraid to stick his neck out when he feels strongly about something.

- Mr Ponsonby looks happy today. Has he got a rich new private patient?
- You've hit the nail on the head. He's got an oil magnate booked in for open-heart surgery at his private clinic.

- You remember the scandal we had over those new filing cabinets. Well, —
- Sorry, I've been away for six months! You'll have to put me in the picture.

- Where's Sally these days?
- She got the sack a week ago. Matron caught her smoking in the ward.

- £30,000 a year as a staff manager! Oh, if only I could get that job!
- Yes, opportunities like that are few and far between.

---

1. Find out what these idioms mean.
2. How would you express these ideas without using an idiom?
3. Write your own dialogues including these idioms correctly and appropriately used.

GIORDANO

UNDERSTANDING THE CASE

Read the case study in the Casebook and answer these questions.

1. How did the Gallery get its name?
2. For what reasons is Jimmie Greenfield to be admired?
3. Why does the Gallery face a 'bleak future'?
4. What kind of relations exist between the Friends of the Giordano and members of the Foundation Trust?
5. What was the most important item on the agenda of the meeting held on 15 April?
6. What factors have contributed to the Foundation's present financial difficulties?
7. Why is it unlikely that a bank can help the Foundation to solve its problems?
8. Outline briefly the different attitudes existing between Dr Tejero and some of the other members of the Board.
9. How should the trustees react to the information contained in the surveyor's report?
10. From the trustees' point of view, which of the four courses of action is probably the easiest and cheapest to put into effect?

VOCABULARY Where's the money going to come from?

Van Huyghens and Donatello are arguing about the Gallery's money problems. Fill in the gaps in their remarks in the usual way.

Van Huyghens Well, if we can't r_____ the money ourselves, we shall have to consider alternative sources of _____. As a museum, we qualify for a government _____, though admittedly it would mean losing our independence. You don't think that's acceptable, I see. Neither do I. That means really that we shall have to find a way to g_____ r_____ the Founder's will. He couldn't have foreseen _____-day conditions, and he made no pr_____ for c_____ like this one. If we are to _____ our _____ problems, we must set up some kind of f_____ which we can draw on in a(n) _____.

Donatello That's an excellent idea! Indeed, I should like to propose that we use the Gallery's _____ resources as investment capital, to buy works by _____ y artists which are likely to a_____ in value. Of course, the market for modern painting is highly _____ve, so I am willing to offer my services to the fund, in an advisory capacity.

Van Huyghens We all know you are a(n) _____, Signor Donatello, and your advice in such a venture would certainly be _____. However, I am afraid we cannot stake the future of the Gallery's ____ss collection on the purchase of paintings which might turn out to be _____. What I had in mind was that the trustees of the Gallery should apply for registration as a _____y. If we have c_____ s_____, we shall enjoy all sorts of advantages . . .

finance	contemporary	authority
fund	current	charity
grant	existing	provision
subsidy	modern	status
	present	
avoid		appreciate
get round	contingency	increase
overcome	emergency	raise
invaluable	charitable	
priceless	financial	
worthless	speculative	

A MUSEUM OF RECORD

Read or listen to the dialogue.

Dr Juan Tejero is on a visit to London. He is now having lunch with two of the Gallery's trustees, Emily Parkinson and Peter Smithson. He is hoping they will support him in his plan to buy the Magnasco painting.

Tejero You go on and on about money, Emily, but I'm only thinking about our reputation. People come to us because we possess a fine and representative collection of seventeenth- and eighteenth-century paintings. Surely, then, we have a duty to acquire the Magnasco.

Parkinson Oh, you've worn me out with your arguments. How about you, Peter?

Smithson I'm absolutely exhausted as well. You're very persistent when you've set your mind on something, Juan.

Tejero Look, I'd like the two of you to do something for me. Go along and view the painting. Perhaps then you'll both be convinced.

Parkinson OK, let's assume we see the work, and we agree with you that it's full of life and movement, the colours are vibrant, its condition is satisfactory and so on—how will that help you? Most of the trustees have strong objections to our purchasing it—however low the price.

Tejero Precisely. That's why I want to ask you both a favour. I wonder if you'd be willing to support me at our next meeting. I shall formally propose we acquire the Magnasco. Emily? Are you going to give me your backing?

Parkinson Oh dear, Juan, you do make life difficult for me.

Tejero You've got to do this for me. You're an authority on Magnasco; people will listen to you. And you, Peter, you mustn't let me down either. I'm counting on you both to be right behind me.

Parkinson I don't know . . .

Smithson It's so difficult to decide. On the one hand, we're desperately short of money; on the other, we have the chance to buy a work of art which would bring a great deal of prestige and glamour to the Gallery . . .

Tejero You really shouldn't hesitate! Listen—let me remind you of what the great Goethe once said. Something like this, I recall: 'Choose well, and your choice will be brief—but endless.'

1 Listen again and find as many expressions as possible which are used to invite people to help you and give you their support.
2 Practise the expressions recorded after the dialogue on the tape.
3 With the following check-list to help you, do the role-playing exercise.

OBTAINING SOMEONE'S COOPERATION

Surely, we have a duty to . . .
I'd like you to do something for me.
I want to ask you a favour/to . . .
I wonder if you'd be willing to . . . ?
Are you going to give me your backing?
You mustn't let me down.
I'm counting on your support/help.
Please do everything possible to help me . . .
I'd very much appreciate it if you could . . .
I should be most grateful if you would . . .

Role-playing exercise

At the meeting of the trustees, it was agreed that members would approach wealthy industrialists, asking them to make donations to the Gallery. Peter Smithson and Emily Parkinson have contacted a Scottish tycoon—the owner of a whisky distillery. This person was extremely cautious when money was mentioned, but he has invited the two trustees to come up to Dundee to have lunch with himself and other members of his board of management. The trustees hope not only to get money from this man but also a promise that he will support a 'Save the Giordano' appeal campaign.

ART LOVERS AND OTHERS

Certain members of the Board of Trustees have been collecting information which they hope will support their demand for the introduction of admission charges. They have now prepared the three charts that you see below. Charts 1 and 2 are based on visitors' answers to a brief questionnaire; Chart 3 is based on the experience of museums and art galleries in various parts of Europe.

Consider what conclusions can be drawn from the charts, and try to answer the questions below them.

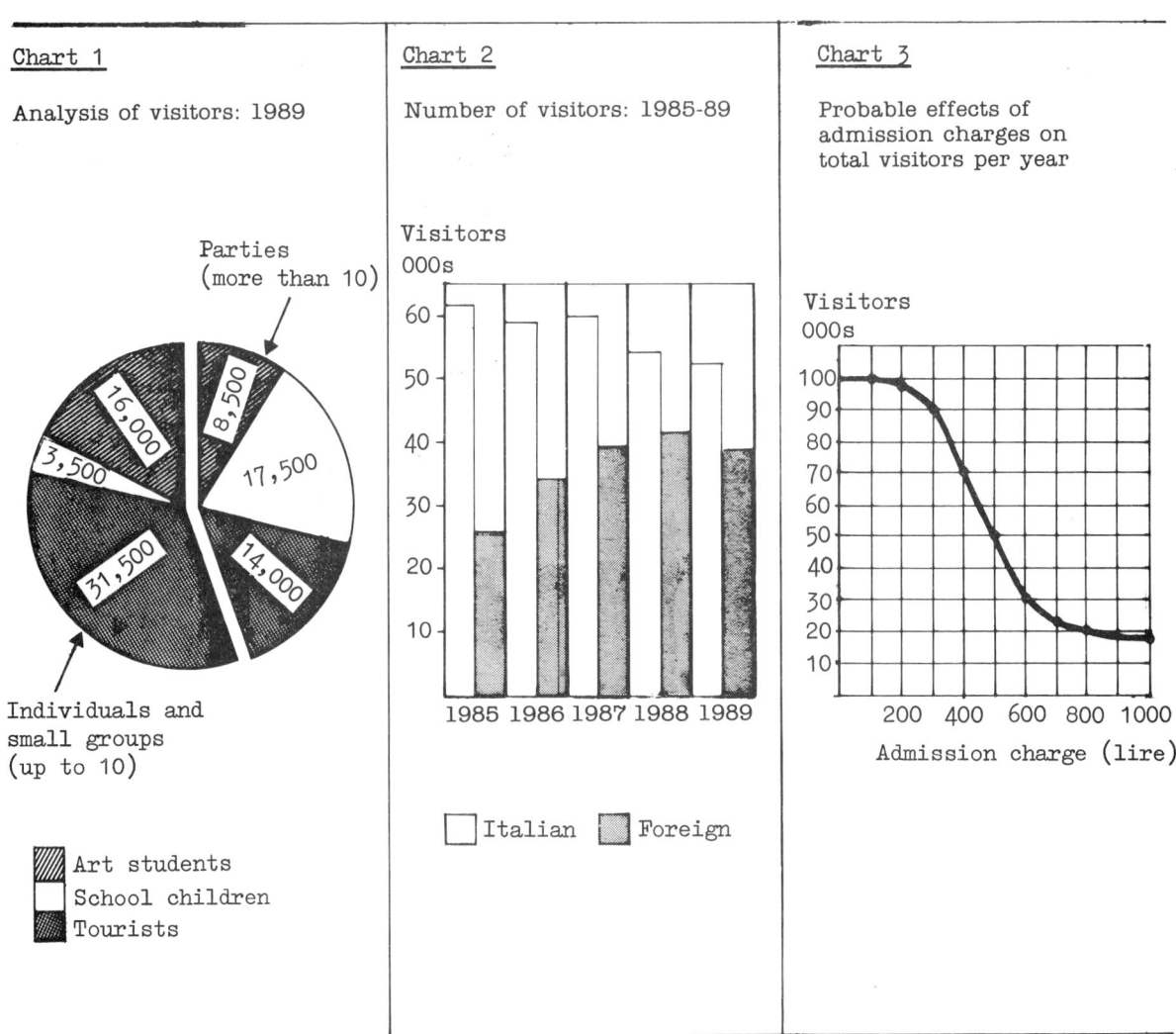

1. What percentage of the Giordano Gallery's income from admission charges would be contributed by (a) tourists (b) art students (c) schoolchildren (d) parties (e) Italians (f) foreigners?

2. If the admission charge was fixed at 500 lire, roughly what income could the Gallery expect?

3. Which types of visitor would decline most sharply if the charge was fixed at 1,000 lire?

4. It is possible to offer reduced charges for children, parties, etc. Suggest a scale of charges which would (a) be acceptable to the public and the trustees (b) maximize the Gallery's income from this source.

THE RIGHT WORDS IN THE RIGHT PLACE

A new Director of the Giordano has been appointed—the former retired through ill health. The new man has a distinguished academic record, but limited experience of running a gallery. To the surprise of the trustees, he has asked them to provide him with a job description. At their next meeting, they find they have considerable difficulty in wording it correctly.

Van Huyghens ... Yes, I agree, Dr Tejero, we should give our new Director, Hugh Youngblood, a very brief description of his responsibilities. We don't want to kill his initiative by putting all kinds of restraints on his powers. Now, would anyone like to offer a description of his main duties?

Parkinson It's simple enough, surely. His main responsibilities are: to acquire paintings for the Gallery, to look after the collections, and to run the Giordano efficiently.

Van Huyghens Any comment?

Donatello Yes, those are the Director's main functions. But I would like to suggest an amendment to Miss Parkinson's wording. Could we not say, 'It is the Director's duty to advise the trustees about acquisitions'? After all, we give final approval.

Parkinson You're quite right, Signor Donatello. How about this, then? 'It is the Director's duty to advise trustees on the growth of the collections.'

Donatello Perfect.

Djilovic And now may I suggest some rephrasing, please. Instead of 'to look after the collections', we could say, 'to undertake the care and display of the collections'. Also, I would replace 'to run the Gallery' with the phrase 'to administer the Gallery and its staff'.

Van Huyghens Good, we're all agreed on those modifications. Any other points?

Guilietta We should also mention the Director will be heavily involved in our building programme.

Van Huyghens Yes, I agree. We could put it this way, 'The Director will have an important role to play in the Gallery's plans for future expansion.' No further comments? Do we need to vote on it? Fine. We can move on to the next item, then.

> Above, in dialogue form, is the discussion relating to this matter. As Secretary to the meeting, it is your task to write the minute for this item of the agenda. A beginning has already been provided. Now, you go on.

The meeting then went on to discuss Mr Youngblood's request that he should be provided with a description of his duties.

WRITTEN ASSIGNMENT

The new Director of the Gallery, Hugh Youngblood, would like to have fuller information about the people visiting the Giordano. Because of the expense, he does not want to commission a market research firm to carry out an elaborate survey. Instead, he has asked an executive in the Gallery's public relations department to draft—in English—a questionnaire which could later be presented to a random sample of visitors. (The document would be translated into several languages.)

> Imagine you are the executive who has been given this job. The Director is allowing you considerable freedom in deciding what questions to include; he simply wants you to gather data about visitors which 'could be useful to the Gallery for future planning'. However, he does have one or two requirements which he has put in a memo to you (see below). Your task now is to design and draft the questionnaire.

In his memo, the Director has stipulated the following:
– The questionnaire should contain 20–30 questions.
– It must provide information concerning: the age, sex, nationality and occupation of visitors; whether they have come as individuals or with a group; how they heard about the Gallery; what their reaction would be if an admission charge was made; what facilities the Gallery should provide which are at present lacking.

A FEW GUIDELINES
Bear in mind these points:

* Phrase each question clearly and precisely, so that it will provide the information you are seeking.

* Do not make any questions too wide in scope. If you do so, the reader will be unsure exactly what information he or she should give.

* Use language the reader will easily understand. Do not be too sophisticated in your choice of structure or vocabulary.

* Consider carefully how you should express certain questions. For example, if you ask the question, *Where do you come from?* do not be surprised if the replies you receive turn out to be less complete and accurate than you would have wished!

* Remember that most of your questions will be aimed at gathering information about the characteristics of the Gallery's visitors, although you may also use the questionnaire to find out their impressions of the collection of paintings.

Alternative assignment

Over the years, a number of people from the US have visited the Giordano Gallery. The trustees are convinced that many Americans would respond to an appeal for funds, and would give generously to help the Gallery overcome its financial problems. They have decided, therefore, to compose a standard letter of appeal, copies of which would be sent to the editors of major newspapers in that country. The letter will stress the US career of the Gallery's founder, Jimmie Greenfield; it will go on to outline the serious financial situation the Gallery now finds itself in, and it will end with an eloquent plea for donations. Your task is to draft this letter.

HEARD ON THE TERRACE

But Dr Tejero... that portrait by Magnasco would fetch at least £50,000!
Chickenfeed, my dear Donatello! Peanuts!

Dr Tejero made out a very good case for buying the painting.
I'd beware of the Doctor if I were you, Miss Eyckhardt. He has the gift of the gab.

Why don't we ask the Friends of the Giordano for a contribution towards the purchase of the painting?
Another contribution? We'd be pushing our luck, don't you think?

May we take the minutes of the last meeting as read?
H'm... Yes...
Good. Let's get down to business then.

Doesn't the Giordano have any picture-restorers on the permanent staff?
No, none. They work on a freelance basis.

I strongly support the idea of a lottery.
Well, I'm utterly opposed to it... and I'll go to any lengths to stop it.

Shortage of cash will limit the scope of your activities, won't it, Professor?
It's bound to. But there are some good projects in the pipeline, and we're going to see those through at any rate.

You're not very happy about the proposal to buy this painting, are you, Miss Campoverdi?
I'm dead against it, and if it goes through I shall have no qualms about calling for Tejero's resignation.

I hear the committee gave you rather a rough ride, Doctor.
Yes! For a while it was touch and go whether I would resign.

That was a stormy meeting, Jose!
The trouble is that whenever we're going through a bad patch, Donatello starts losing his nerve.

1. Find out what these idioms mean.
2. How would you express these ideas without using an idiom?
3. Write your own dialogues including these idioms correctly and appropriately used.

COCONUT GROVE

UNDERSTANDING THE CASE

Read the case study in the Casebook and answer these questions.

1 Where is the Coconut Grove Hotel located?
2 What are some of the hotel's outstanding features?
3 Who (a) owns the hotel (b) manages it (c) cooks the meals (d) gives legal advice to its owner?
4 What evidence is there to suggest that the owner does not take as much interest in his hotel as he should?
5 How does Dick Jeffries react to the information Paul Drew gives him concerning his bar employees?
6 What made Paul Drew suspect that Sammy Hall was dishonest and what finally convinced him of this fact?
7 How did Norman the barman let down his fellow employees?
8 Why didn't Dick Jeffries immediately dismiss his manager Sammy Hall when he became sure this employee was cheating him?
9 In what way does the presence of Mrs Singh in the hotel complicate Dick Jeffries' decision?
10 Should the information given by Paula Jeffries in the final paragraph have any bearing on her husband's final decision in this matter? Give reasons for your answer.

VOCABULARY The man who made it pay

Sammy Hall, on a quiet evening in the hotel bar, is revealing to a guest the truth behind the Coconut Grove's success. Fill in the gaps in his remarks in the usual way.

Sammy Listen, I'll tell you. Twenty years ago this place was nothing. The only _____ activity was selling coconuts that fell off trees. Then came Independence! The Vanilla Government decided to d___y the economy, start p_____ the tourist t_____. Mr Jeffries took this bit of land from the Government in 1970, on a fourteen-year l_____. Now he o_____ the f___ h__.

How do you think he made all that money?

When I came to this hotel in 1973, it was nothing. Buying the p_____, renovating the place, buying all the f_____ and f_____, had taken every cent Mr Jeffries could lay his hands on. The i_____ from the hotel barely c_____ his o_____.

The guests stole the ashtrays and never paid their bills, and the c_____ were ringing up every other day and threatening l_____ a_____. The Coconut Grove's only a_____ were the blue sky and the golden sand. Everything else was a l_____.

But as soon as I saw this place, I knew it had terrific p_____. An unspoilt tropical paradise! I passed the word around to a few of the boys in New York, Chicago, Miami. Suddenly we're p_____, we're booked up solid right through the s_____. The bank b_____ is in the black again and Mr Jeffries is making a f_____. Well, he's worked for it, I guess. But he o_____ a little bit of it to me, too. I tell you, when I started here there was *nothing* ...

diversify	fittings	action
promote	fixtures	creditor
prosperous	freehold	season
	lease	
business	premises	
commercial		
legal	asset	
trade	balance	
	fortune	
cover	income	
owe	liability	
own	potential	
	overheads	

47

IDEAL FOR HONEYMOONERS

Read or listen to the dialogue.

Dick Jeffries has applied for permission to build an annexe to his hotel. Time has passed, but he still has not had the plans approved. So he arranges a meeting with Mrs Paula Knight, an official from the Ministry dealing with the application.

Jeffries I know you'll think I'm impatient, Mrs Knight, but I'm beginning to get really worried about the delay in getting my plans approved. Is there any hitch; something I don't know about? Does anyone object to what I want to do?

Knight Not that I know of. It's just that the approval procedure takes time. For one thing, we've had to ask the fishermen who have houses near you whether they have any objection. Don't forget, you're the only hotel on the edge of the beach in that area.

Jeffries That shouldn't take long, surely. The fishermen are good friends of mine.

Knight Normally, it wouldn't take so long, but you seem to forget we've also had the carnival. Most of our staff take a couple of weeks off for that, and they usually need another week to recuperate!

Jeffries Yes, I rather thought that might be the reason for the delay. Tell me one thing, Mrs Knight. Can I take it that your people approve the scheme in principle?

Knight Well, let's just say that most of the committee members—the planning committee that is—have seen your plans and have raised no strong objection. Mind you, one or two were worried about the height of the building.

Jeffries It won't be more than sixteen metres high, and the frontage will be about forty metres. That's acceptable, isn't it?

Knight I think so. The point is, we don't want the annexe to stick out like a sore thumb. It's got to blend with the environment—not dominate it.

Jeffries Well, I must admit, there aren't many tall buildings along the edge of the beach.

Knight Yes, and this one will be closer than any other.

Jeffries That's because I want the annexe to be well away from the hotel. I hope the suites will be used mainly by honeymoon couples looking for a bit of peace and quiet—and a romantic atmosphere, of course.

Knight It's not that noisy at the Coconut Grove, is it?

Jeffries It can be rather lively, especially if Sammy—he's my manager—starts trying to show the guests how to do the limbo.

Knight Oh, Sammy Hall! I know him. Absolutely charming, isn't he?

1 Listen again and find as many expressions as possible which are used to ask someone to approve a project or an idea.
2 Practise the expressions recorded after the dialogue on the tape.
3 With the following check-list to help you, do the role-playing exercise.

GETTING APPROVAL FOR A PROJECT

Does anyone object to what I want to do?

Do they have any objection to . . . ?

Can I take it you approve the scheme in principle?

No one's raised any strong objection, have they?

That's acceptable, isn't it?

Do you approve of . . . ?

Are you all in favour of . . . ?

Do you all agree with me that . . . ?

So you think this is basically a good idea?

Is everyone happy about . . . ?

Role-playing exercise

Some time ago, Dick Jeffries asked Sammy Hall to think of ways to make the hotel more profitable. Sammy agreed to do this. Actually, however, he already has a project in mind. He wants to open a discotheque on the hotel's premises. This kind of club, where young people could dance to the latest pop music, would be easy to run and a real money-spinner—so he believes. It would also have the advantage of keeping Sammy in touch with the fun-loving younger generation of the island.

The opportunity to put forward his scheme comes when he is having a drink on the hotel terrace with Dick Jeffries, Paul Drew and Sharma Singh. Sammy is confident that Sharma will approve of his project, but what about the others?

CRIME DOESN'T PAY

Sammy Hall controls the illicit buying and selling of alcohol at the Coconut Grove himself. Soft drinks, however, are less profitable and less risky so he lets Norman and Daryl, the barmen, run their own 'business' in these, taking as his share only 10 per cent of their profits.

Norman and Daryl usually buy their stock in small quantities from different retailers. They buy a total of about V$1,000 worth of soft drinks each month. Now, however, the high season is coming and Norman decides to stock up. Yesterday, without saying anything to Sammy or Daryl, he drove the pick-up into town and brought back a big consignment from a cash-and-carry warehouse near the docks. Here's the invoice that he received.

He was very pleased with himself, as they did not usually manage to get any discount on their relatively small purchases and they would make a sizeable profit on the bar tariff.

When Daryl saw the invoice, however, he nearly hit the ceiling; 'You idiot!' he said. 'That's far too much. We can't shift that lot in less than three months—Jeffries is bound to suspect something.' When Sammy Hall saw the loaded pick-up, he too was very unhappy.

'You boys have been paying me ten per cent of your takings to keep the store-room door open and my mouth shut,' he said. 'Well, if you want me to turn a blind eye to this lot, from now on it'll be twenty per cent—OK?'

```
                        QUICKFIZZ & Co.

                        Invoice 524/81

Fruit juices, assorted  288 doz. at V$7.20         2,073.60
Blik-Cola, 225g cans    216 doz. at V$6.60         1,425.60
Split tonic              40 doz. at V$6.00           240.00
                                                   _____
                                                   3,739.20
                        Less 33.3% trade discount  1,246.40
                                                   _____
                                                V$ 2,492.80
                                                   _____
```

```
                   TARIFF

        Fruit juices       V$ 1.20

        Blik-Cola          V$ 1.10

        Tonic, etc.        V$ 1.00
```

Consider and estimate the answers to these questions:

1 What is the mark-up on soft drinks sold in the bar? (We can assume that wholesale prices are the same all over the island.) How much profit did Norman himself hope to make during the next month, after paying all expenses, and assuming that he sold all the new stock?

2 If Daryl is right about the quantity they can actually sell in a month and if Sammy insists on the increased percentage of 'hush money', how much extra will Norman actually make in the coming month compared with his normal profit on V$1,000 worth of stock?

3 Which of these figures most closely represents the commission Sammy is likely to have received on the normal V$1,000 per month consignment—V$80, V$110 or V$160?

THE RIGHT WORDS IN THE RIGHT PLACE

Like many people in positions of power, Dick Jeffries would be powerless without someone in his outer office to organize his working day and tell him what to do next. This is his faithful secretary Edwina, who can even make sense of the messages he records on his dictating machine.

> Below, you will see the word-for-word transcript of a memo dictated by Jeffries and the start of Edwina's typed version. Write the whole memo as she wrote it.

Jeffries Er . . . now this is to everyone on the staff of the hotel, from me. Sorry, I mean from the Proprietor. It's about security. I'll leave you to word it properly. To be exact, it's about the security of guests' property and—er—belongings.

Um . . . Well, what I want to say is that we've had a few problems lately with people, guests that is, losing things from their rooms. This is a very serious matter because word gets around very quickly about these things and—er—the management views this development with profound alarm. Now then. This is what we're going to do—

First, all locks on guest-room doors are being changed. As from Sunday 26 October, master keys will only be held by Room Service (they'll have six of them), the General Manager, the Safety and Security Officer, and myself, with one spare in the Emergency cupboard in Reception.

Second, we've put notices about this in all the rooms—about looking after your valuables, I mean—notices in all the rooms, telling guests that if they don't want their stuff to be pinched they should hand it over to Reception for safekeeping.

Third, I'd like everyone to remember that it's up to them to blow the whistle on any suspicious-looking characters they see hanging around the place.

Er . . . that's about it, I guess, Edwina. If you can just type that up for me in decent English, I'll initial it when I get back tomorrow and we can get it sent round.

From   Proprietor
To   All members of staff
Date   23 October 19 _

Security of Valuables in Guest Rooms

1 It has come to my notice that there have recently been a number of complaints about the disappearance of valuable items from guest rooms.

WRITTEN ASSIGNMENT

> Imagine that you are Sammy Hall, the Manager of the Coconut Grove. You are convinced that the hotel has tremendous potential as a conference centre. Mr Jeffries, though he seems sceptical, has asked you to give him your ideas in a written report.

GETTING THE FACTS

The case study contains a lot of information about the hotel, but Sammy Hall also knows, from his own experience:

(a) that it can accommodate 250 people, in single or double rooms;
(b) that bookings throughout the year average 85 per cent of capacity;
(c) that the restaurant and other public rooms are at present used to about 45 per cent capacity;
(d) that a conference centre needs to accommodate at least 100 people to be viable—and they want to enjoy themselves as well as to work;
(e) that more and more large organizations want to hold conferences in places like Vanilla. The conference is also a holiday, a way of rewarding good employees.

WHAT IS NEEDED?

What additional accommodation, facilities and staff will the Coconut Grove need? You need not be too exact in your answers, but give estimates which are numerical, not vague—e.g. *up to 100 new beds*, not *a lot of new beds*.

PRESENTATION

Keep in mind the conventional pattern of the business report (see Appendix, section 4), but make the pattern fit the material. Your findings will be short, but you will have many recommendations to make.

(a) *Title: Report on proposed . . .* or simply *Proposals . . .*
(b) *Terms of reference*: remember that Mr Jeffries asked you to write the report after you suggested setting up a conference centre.
(c) *Procedure*: probably none at all, unless you have discussed your ideas with architects, lawyers, conference organizers, or anyone else who can offer expert advice.
(d) *Findings*: don't waste time telling Mr Jeffries facts about the hotel which he already knows. Just say:
   (i) why you think there would be a good demand for a conference centre in Vanilla;
   (ii) why the Coconut Grove is a good place to start one.

(e) *Conclusions* and *Recommendations*: this is the most important section of the report, so plan it carefully. Sort out your ideas and classify them in accordance with a plan, e.g.:
   New buildings
   Alterations to existing buildings
   New facilities
   Extra staff
   etc. . . .

Finally, sum up your argument in one or two sentences. Remember, you are trying to persuade Mr Jeffries to adopt your idea; you must make it sound convincing and attractive.

Alternative assignment

Jean Pinot, the Personnel Manager of Bonhomme (based in Paris), has to organize a conference of his company's representatives and agents—about 80 people altogether. Where shall it be? He racks his brains. Inspiration! That Caribbean paradise that his cousin stayed at last year and has raved about ever since. Information is required at once, and if possible a provisional booking must be made. The matter is urgent. He has instructed you, a member of his staff, to telex the Coconut Grove at once. Draft the message you will send.

HEARD ON THE QUAYSIDE

We've got to be careful how we handle this business with Sammy.
Mmm. The reputation of the hotel is at stake.

Listen: take my advice and don't rock the boat.
You mean . . . forget that Paul ever told me anything was wrong?

But do you have any proof of this?
Oh yes. Norman gave the game away.

Shrewd fellow, Paul Drew.
Smart as they come. You won't pull the wool over *his* eyes.

You seem to be raking it in these days, Dick.
Well, it's true up to a point. We've certainly been making a bomb on the restaurant.

Sammy's the ideal hotel manager!
Well, in some ways. For instance, he's extrovert, sociable—a real live wire.

Why on earth did anyone let that loudmouth into the cabaret last night? How did he get past Sammy?
Well, Sammy saw he was sloshed . . . He was going to throw him out. But the guy pulled a fast one on him . . . told him he was the Prime Minister's nephew!

You mean Paul tricked Norman into confessing?
Well, it was no use asking him point blank. The boy would have simply denied it.

I'm surprised the Drum Hotel is still open, especially at this time of the year.
Apparently, they've decided to keep a skeleton staff in case they get a few late holiday-makers. Trying to hedge their bets, I suppose.

Darling, how about taking me out to dinner tonight at the Coconut Grove?
What! They make you pay through the nose at that place . . .

1 Find out what these idioms mean.
2 How would you express these ideas without using an idiom?
3 Write your own dialogues including these idioms correctly and appropriately used.

TUMBRIL

UNDERSTANDING THE CASE
Read the case study in the Casebook and answer these questions.

1. What sort of book does Tumbril publish? What advantages does the firm gain from specialization?
2. 'There is still a family atmosphere in the organization.' What are likely to be the advantages and disadvantages of this?
3. Who is ultimately responsible for making the major management decisions at Tumbril?
4. Why did Tumbril's last visit to the Frankfurt Book Fair turn out rather differently from what they had expected?
5. What is unusual about publishers' relationships with their agents overseas?
6. How do Jonathan and Richard's views appear to differ concerning the ideal agent for Tumbril?
7. How should Richard have acted when the American expressed interest in acquiring the agency for Tumbril?
8. If the American keeps his promise about the volume of Tumbril's European business in the next two years, how much will Gumpi make in agent's commissions?
9. What advantages does Gumpi offer that van Brasil does not?
10. Is Richard justified in being 'thoroughly upset' by the letter he receives on 1 October?

VOCABULARY How did it happen?

Peter Stoddart, representing another publishing house, is chatting to Johan van Brasil about Tumbril. Fill in the gaps in his remarks with words from the box.

Stoddart ... They're t_____ of a lot of highly r_____ old family businesses in Britain. They sometimes l_____ management e_____ when they have to t_____ unfamiliar problems but their intentions are excellent.

Tumbril almost went out of business in the late fifties. Then the company started to f_____ again in the 1960s, when new universities and colleges were m_____ all over the country. They took a_____ of the huge demand for books for these new institutions. As a result, they now have a h_____ bank balance and a t_____ business, even though their decision-making is a bit ____ing in s_____ still.

The danger with old family firms is that sometimes there may be no clear _____-chart, no chain of _____. It's sometimes hard to tell who is r_____ for what, and who he r_____ to. When things go well, you have a very pleasant a_____ and m_____ is high, but when something goes wrong there can be confusion and bad f_____.

healthy	atmosphere	command
reputable	feeling	order
responsible	morale	organization
thriving	sophistication	
typical		advantage
	lack	expertise
flourish	lacking	
mushroom	tackle	
report		
vet		

52

ADVICE FROM A CHARTERED ACCOUNTANT

Read or listen to the dialogue.

Richard and Jonathan Tumbril seek the advice of a local chartered accountant, Louise Bayliss. She suggests they should strengthen their management team.

Richard So you think I'm losing my grip, do you?

Louise Now, don't you go putting words in my mouth, Richard. All I'm saying is that you need more management, especially in the financial field. Your turnover's shooting up, you're expanding overseas, you're going to be negotiating with agents and distributors . . .

Jonathan OK, you want us to hire a Financial Director. Is that it?

Louise Exactly. If you got someone to handle the company's financial affairs, that would leave you, Richard, to concentrate on building up the list of titles, negotiating with authors and so on; you, Jonathan, could then spend more time on marketing. At the moment, you're both trying to do too much and often duplicating work.

Richard It's a very interesting idea—bringing someone in from outside the company—but I'm not sure a new man or post would solve our problems. What do you think, Jonathan?

Jonathan I don't think I really like the idea, frankly, Louise. As you know, Richard and I have had a few misunderstandings recently. Now, if a new person came in, virtually equal to us in status, decision-making would be even harder . . . and slower.

Louise Ah, maybe that would be a good thing. If you had to consult a third person, you wouldn't act so hastily at times.

Richard We take the point, Louise! I certainly hope we never mess things up again as we did with Gumpi. Even so, I'm not convinced a Financial Director is what we want. You know what they say: 'Two's company, three's a crowd.'

Louise OK, I grant you there's the possibility of a personality clash, or that two of you might gang up on the third. So, you could have an understanding with whoever you hired, that if things didn't work out, he or she would leave.

Richard No, I'm sorry, Louise. I just don't think we need some high-powered outsider at present . . .

Jonathan I'm not entirely convinced either. As it is, our responsibilities overlap a great deal. If we brought in a third person, there'd be a lot of confusion, no one knowing who was responsible for what.

Louise OK, you win. But let's see in a couple of years' time, when your overseas operation is in full swing. It'll be a different story then.

1 Listen again and find as many expressions as possible which are used to reject a person's advice or suggestions.

2 Practise the expressions recorded after the dialogue on the tape.

3 With the following check-list to help you, do the role-playing exercise.

REJECTING ADVICE/TURNING DOWN OFFERS

It's a very interesting idea, but I don't think it would work in practice.
I don't think I really like the idea, frankly.
Even so, I'm not convinced that . . .
No, I'm sorry, I just don't think . . .
I'm not totally convinced by your arguments, quite honestly.
I really can't go along with . . ., I'm afraid.
I'm not in favour of . . . at all.
It's all very well to suggest ——ing, but that would . . .
No, I don't agree with you at all about . . .
No, it's out of the question.

Role-playing exercise

Don and Wilma Freeman are sociologists from the United States currently teaching in Britain. They have submitted to Tumbril a manuscript provisionally entitled *USA: a Nation in Decline*. The book is brilliantly written, but neither Jonathan nor Richard—both very pro-American—like its message. Essentially, its theme is that present-day US civilization is 'barbaric', and that the nation is declining economically, socially, politically and morally. The Freemans are now at Tumbril trying to persuade Jonathan and Richard to take the book. These two are fairly sure they will reject the manuscript—unless the US academics produce some powerful arguments.

A BOOK FOR THE POCKET—OR THE COFFEE TABLE?

Alice Marker is the Arts and Crafts Editor of Tumbril. One important book that she is handling at present is a well-written, authoritative account of the history and techniques of Japanese gardening.

This book would make a useful addition to Tumbril's paperback series on *The Techniques of the Fine Arts*. Books in this series are illustrated with a few black-and-white photographs only. However, Alice is certain that *Japanese Gardening* would be very successful as a de luxe edition, with a fine binding and colour illustrations on every page. She has drawn up some estimated costings:

	Paperback	De luxe
Print run	20,000 copies	5,000? (Might reprint quickly if successful)
Production cost (printing and binding)	£10,000	At least £30,000 – perhaps more
Distribution (including advertising)	£2,500 at most	£3,000? £5,000?
Notes Market	* Mainly in UK * Easy to reach * Little competition * Discriminating, specialist reader * Series well known	* Worldwide * Difficult to reach * Much competition from 'glossy' art books * Less discriminating buyer
Price range	£2.50 – £3.00	£10 – £18

Consider Alice's estimates and say in which format you consider the book should be published. You may prefer to reserve judgement on the format until you have considered the retail price at which the book should be sold. The author will take 10 per cent of the retail price as his royalty, and the bookseller will take 33⅓ per cent as his profit on the sale. Should Alice aim to sell the book at the upper or the lower end of the price ranges shown in her notes?

THE RIGHT WORDS IN THE RIGHT PLACE

Last March, the editorial department of an expanding publishing company moved to larger premises. When the recently recruited Editor of Children's Publications returns from a holiday abroad, he cannot find an original manuscript—and copy—entrusted to him by an author, André Crivain. This person is living at present in the South of France. While the Editor plays for time and desperately tries to track down the missing material, Crivain becomes increasingly anxious and alarmed.

APRIL

10 (Crivain writes from St Tropez, France)

You have had my manuscripts since February—surely long enough to make an assessment. Kindly return the material at your earliest convenience. By the way, a French editor has read a synopsis of the work, and he seems very interested. Maybe this delay has been for the best.

14 (The Editor replies)

We have by no means lost enthusiasm for your most interesting MS. Please leave it with us a few weeks longer—and be patient.

19 (Crivain writes from St Tropez)

I'm afraid I cannot agree to your request, although I'm flattered by what you say about my work. Please send the manuscript and copy by return of post.

25 (Crivain sends a cable)

WHERE IS MY MS STOP CALL ME SOONEST STOP

28 (The Editor phones Crivain)

I'm very sorry I didn't call you earlier, Monsieur. I've been abroad for a few days... You're worried because you don't have another copy of the book. My goodness! Hmm... we really must get that manuscript back to you then. If I were you, in future, I'd make copies of what I'd written—just to be on the safe side... Sorry for all the inconvenience. My secretary would normally have looked after the matter, but she's been on her back for the last two weeks—slipped disc or something.

29 (The Editor talks to the superintendent who was in charge of the relocation)

Not much chance of seeing those manuscripts again, I'm afraid, sir. A lot of stuff got thrown away during the changeover. Everything was so chaotic, the porters were going out of their minds, what with the pressure and the hours of overtime they were doing.

30 (A director of the company calls the Children's Editor)

A Monsieur Crivain has just called me from St Tropez. Now what on earth is going on?... What's that?... Well, I want a report at once—with all the facts!

> Using the information given in the extracts, write the Editor's report for the Director, explaining why the manuscripts got lost and summarizing the company's dealings with Crivain.

WRITTEN ASSIGNMENT

Three junior executives at Tumbril are being given a thorough training in all aspects of the publishing business. As part of their programme, Richard Tumbril arranged to send them on an editing course. It was to have begun on 28 February. Richard has just received a letter informing him the course has been postponed for a month. It will now start on 28 March. 'Well, the boys are going to be disappointed,' thinks Richard. The new date means that the course will be in the week preceding the Didacta Book Fair. Everyone in the company will be very busy preparing for this event and the executives will be expected to give a helping hand. Richard must now send the three persons concerned a memo telling them they cannot go on the course.

> Draft this memo for Richard. Make sure you break the news to the executives as politely as possible, and reassure them they will be given the opportunity to attend a similar course in the near future. (Notes on memo writing are given in Appendix, section 2.)

Alternative assignment

Herr Franz Zimmermann is Managing Director of a German educational publishing company which is located in West Germany. Zimmermann has heard —through the grapevine—that Tumbril are having all kinds of difficulties with their agent, the Gumpi company. Since he has been keen for some time to represent a British educational publisher, Zimmermann feels he must not let slip this opportunity to step in and propose that his company should take over the Tumbril agency in West Germany.

He will now write to Richard Tumbril, whom he has met casually at various book fairs, and mention his interest in becoming the British company's agent. He will try to convince Richard of his serious intentions by giving plenty of information in the letter. He will talk about himself, his company (size, turnover, workforce, range of activities etc.), his sales organization, and his capabilities as agent. He will end by suggesting a meeting to discuss his proposal in greater detail.

Imagine you are Franz Zimmermann. Write to Richard Tumbril proposing your company as agent.

HEARD OUTSIDE THE BOARD ROOM

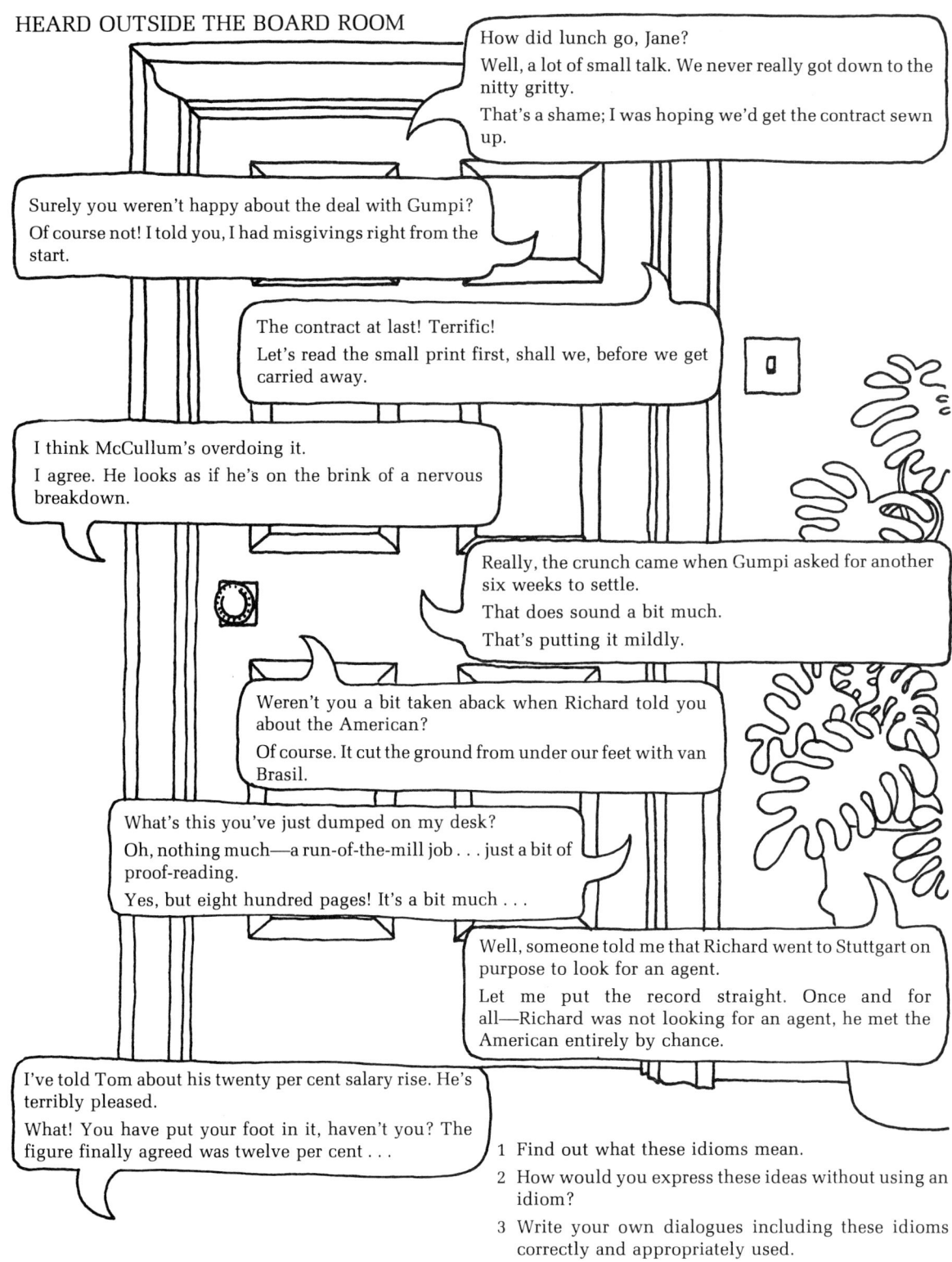

How did lunch go, Jane?
Well, a lot of small talk. We never really got down to the nitty gritty.
That's a shame; I was hoping we'd get the contract sewn up.

Surely you weren't happy about the deal with Gumpi?
Of course not! I told you, I had misgivings right from the start.

The contract at last! Terrific!
Let's read the small print first, shall we, before we get carried away.

I think McCullum's overdoing it.
I agree. He looks as if he's on the brink of a nervous breakdown.

Really, the crunch came when Gumpi asked for another six weeks to settle.
That does sound a bit much.
That's putting it mildly.

Weren't you a bit taken aback when Richard told you about the American?
Of course. It cut the ground from under our feet with van Brasil.

What's this you've just dumped on my desk?
Oh, nothing much—a run-of-the-mill job . . . just a bit of proof-reading.
Yes, but eight hundred pages! It's a bit much . . .

Well, someone told me that Richard went to Stuttgart on purpose to look for an agent.
Let me put the record straight. Once and for all—Richard was not looking for an agent, he met the American entirely by chance.

I've told Tom about his twenty per cent salary rise. He's terribly pleased.
What! You have put your foot in it, haven't you? The figure finally agreed was twelve per cent . . .

1 Find out what these idioms mean.
2 How would you express these ideas without using an idiom?
3 Write your own dialogues including these idioms correctly and appropriately used.

Hi-Flite

UNDERSTANDING THE CASE

Read the case study in the Casebook and answer these questions.

1. Who does Bascombe report to?
2. Who reports to Bascombe? To Landon?
3. What happens to a piece of furniture when it has been sold?
4. What advantages did the management hope to gain by putting the furniture department on the ground floor?
5. Why are delays in the delivery of furniture so frequent and so long?
6. If a customer telephones the store with a serious complaint, who should he speak to?
7. Why is the Store Manager so alarmed by the number of customers' complaints?
8. Why is there friction between the Transport Manager and the Loading Bay Supervisor?
9. Why is there a high staff turnover in some departments?
10. What sort of changes could the Store Manager probably make on his own authority? What sort would require authorization from Head Office?

VOCABULARY How it works—in theory and practice

Mr Bascombe is explaining the workings of his section to his new clerical assistant, Joseph Adewale. Fill in the gaps in his remarks with words from the box.

Bascombe Now then, I'll tell you all about how we d_____ to customers. Every day at 1700 hours precisely I go through the i_____ that have come in from the sales departments, and I make up the lorry-_____ ready for the next day. All the i_____ that are going to one particular area go in the same v_____. Next morning, the porters receive their instructions from me and proceed to l_____ the items into the _____. Then the d_____ and their m_____ come along, and they _____ the stuff to the customers. At least, that's what's supposed to happen.

One of our problems is that we've got no m_____ _____g equipment for heavy stuff. Everything has to be moved by _____, and the staff aren't trained for it. They're working here in a very confined _____, and there's never enough _____ to stack everything. Proper s_____ f_____ would be a big help. But the biggest help of all would be if that silly little man Landon would stop filling this _____ up with furniture all the time.

Next, packing. Small or fragile items are packed in c_____ or c_____ boxes. Larger pieces, if they have to go a long way, may be p_____ in wooden c_____.

deliver	facility	driver
despatch	place	hand
handle	room	invoice
load	space	mate
	storage	mechanical
goods		
item	cardboard	
	carton	
truck	crate	
van	pack	
vehicle	package	
	packaging	

A CUSTOMER'S COMPLAINT

Read or listen to the dialogue.
In this dialogue, one of Hi-Flite's customers, Mr Wilkins, calls the company's Head Office to make a complaint.

Secretary Good afternoon. Managing Director's office.
Wilkins Afternoon. I'd like to make a complaint, please, to the Managing Director. What is his name, by the way?
Secretary Mr Fuller, sir, but I'm afraid he's not available at the moment. Perhaps I can be of assistance.
Wilkins No, miss, I'm afraid you can't. I don't like having to complain, but I've had a lot of trouble with your company, one way and another. I'm going right to the top this time.
Secretary Oh dear—I am sorry. Let me transfer you to our Complaints Department—
Wilkins I've already spoken to the Complaints Department. This really isn't good enough. Look—are you going to put me through to the Managing Director or aren't you?
Secretary Very well, sir. What name is it, please?
Wilkins My name's Wilkins.
Secretary Will you hold on a moment please, Mr Wilkins?
 . . . Mr Fuller, there's a Mr Wilkins on the line. He's very dissatisfied with the service we've given him. He's really very angry.
Fuller OK, Susan, put him through.
 . . . Hello, Fuller speaking. Mr Wilkins? I gather you've been having a spot of bother.
Wilkins Well, I suppose you can call it a spot of bother if you like. I call it a downright scandal, and I'm not going to put up with it any longer.
Fuller That sounds bad. Can you give me the details?
Wilkins Well, six weeks ago, I bought a bedroom suite from your store in North London. I was promised delivery within three days. Over a week later, a van arrived at my house—with the wrong goods. It took another two weeks for them to sort that out.
Fuller I see. Well, we must look into that.
Wilkins Oh, that's not all. The next time your people came, one man dropped his end of the wardrobe. Bang went one of the doors. So that had to go back for a replacement. That was three weeks ago and I'm still waiting!
Fuller Oh dear, this is really very serious . . .
Wilkins I'm glad you think so. I'm absolutely disgusted with the way I've been treated by your company. But what are you going to do about it, Mr—er—Fuller?
Fuller I'm going to make some enquiries right away, then ring you back when I've sorted things out. I'm really very sorry, Mr Wilkins, for all the trouble you've had. It's not the way we like to do things . . .

1 Listen again and find as many expressions as possible which are used to show dissatisfaction with goods or services you have received.
2 Practise the expressions recorded after the dialogue on the tape.
3 With the following check-list to help you, do the role-playing exercise.

COMPLAINING ABOUT GOODS OR SERVICES

I'd like to make a complaint, please.
I don't like to complain, but I've had a lot of trouble with . . .
This kind of service just isn't good enough.
I'm very dissatisfied with . . .
I'm not going to put up with . . .
Now, you listen to me. I'm disgusted with the way I've been treated.
I'm not the sort of person who normally complains, but . . .
I'm sorry. I'm not at all satisfied with . . .
Look, I'm very unhappy about the way I'm being treated.
Frankly, I'm very annoyed about . . .

Role-playing exercise

Almost six months ago, a company which supplies houseplants and 'indoor gardens' for smart offices installed an elaborate display of growing plants in the reception hall of Hi-Flite's Head Office in Birmingham. Now, all these plants have died. John Fuller, Hi-Flite's Managing Director, is furious, and his secretary, Susan, whose job it is to look after them, is very upset. Fuller has called the suppliers several times, asking for someone to come and look at the plants, but no one has shown up. Finally, today, the company's Service Manager and a salesman are coming to discuss the matter. Fuller wants to get his money back. The two representatives from the suppliers will try to lay the blame on the secretary—if they can.

HOW FAR AND HOW LONG?

Coldstream is not the only Hi-Flite manager with storage problems, and at Head Office in Birmingham they are thinking seriously about setting up a system of warehouses from which goods could be quickly distributed to stores. This would release a lot of space in the stores which is now used for keeping unsold stock.

There are two possible locations for warehouses, marked 1 and 2 on the map. Both have good road and rail links and room for indefinite expansion. Hi-Flite's directors and senior management, however, are split down the middle on one major issue: should they have two big warehouses or one enormous one?

If they have two warehouses, each one will be within easy reach of one or more of their biggest suppliers. If they have only one, administration and stock control become simpler and the firm will benefit from economies of scale.

In making the final decision, the Board will naturally give great weight to fuel costs and journey times for their fleet of trucks. The map will help you to advise the Board on these.

Study the map carefully and estimate some of the distances between warehouses and locations of stores. Then answer these questions:

1. If only one warehouse is developed, what will be the maximum distance and travelling time to a Hi-Flite branch? (Trucks average 80 kph.)
2. If two warehouses are developed, what will be the average time and distance for a journey to a branch?
3. What advice would you give the Board?

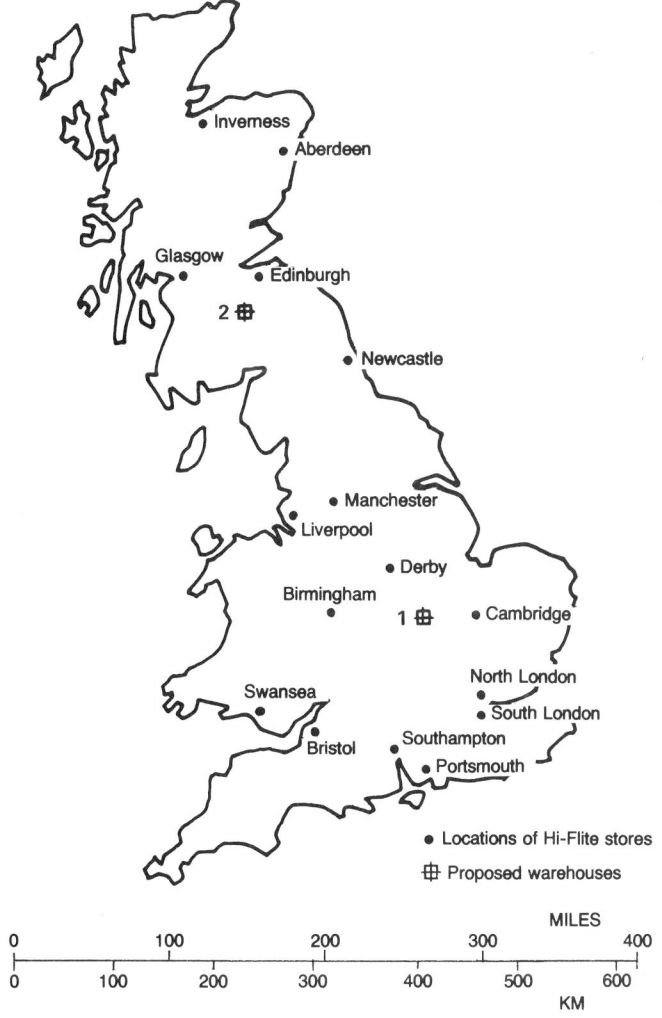

THE RIGHT WORDS IN THE RIGHT PLACE

> As soon as he has put the phone down after his call to Birmingham, Mr Wilkins begins to write a letter to John Fuller, giving details of his complaint about the furniture which has still not arrived. Below, there is an expanded version of what he said on the telephone. Your task is to write the letter. The calendar is put in to help you work out the dates.

Wilkins ... Well, I bought the stuff on the nineteenth of February—a bedroom suite, *Windsor*, yes, that was the name of the range. I've got the invoice here: number 301752. Five hundred and thirty-seven pounds. I signed the hire-purchase agreement, do you want the particulars? No? ... OK then, I'll tell you what happened, blow by blow. They said I'd get the goods by Saturday. Well, I waited till the following Wednesday and then I called the assistant who'd sold me the suite. His name's Johnson, M. B. Johnson, I've got his card here which he gave me. He said he'd look into it urgently. So on the Monday—that would be ... mmm ... let's see, March the second, two of your chaps brought a bedroom suite to my house, and of course, it wasn't the right one. So I told them to take it back again. I called the Sales Manager the next day and she said she was very sorry, the mistake would be rectified immediately, et cetera, et cetera ... Huh! more than two weeks I waited! They managed to come again on the twentieth, that was a Friday. It was then that they dropped the wardrobe and smashed one of the doors. I couldn't get the Sales Manager that time, so I had a little chat with Mr Johnson again. I was rather annoyed, I'm afraid, but I explained to him it was nothing personal ... He swore there'd be a replacement wardrobe in my bedroom by Wednesday evening—the twenty-fifth of March. I even checked with the Transport Manager a day or two later. Well, that was two weeks ago—and I'm still waiting! Now, look here, Mr—er—Fuller, I expect you to do something about this state of affairs—quick!

			February			
*S	M	T	W	Th	F	S
1	2	3	4	5	6	7
8	9	10	11	12	13	14
15	16	17	18	19	20	21
22	23	24	25	26	27	28
			March			
*S	M	T	W	Th	F	S
1	2	3	4	5	6	7
8	9	10	11	12	13	14
15	16	17	18	19	20	21
22	23	24	25	26	27	28
29	30	31				

*No Deliveries

WRITTEN ASSIGNMENT

> John Fuller, the Managing Director of Hi-Flite, calls for a report from Jeffrey Coldstream on the storage and delivery of furniture in the North London store. Write Coldstream's report for him. Say what action you and your colleagues have taken, and what further recommendations you wish to make.

LAYOUT AND PRESENTATION
Copies of this report will probably be circulated to several people in Head Office, but Coldstream doesn't know exactly who. Therefore, he will probably not present it as a memo; he will simply give it a title (*Report on* . . .) and send it to Fuller with a brief covering letter attached to it. This will simply say: *Here is the report which you asked for, and which I hope you will find useful.*

Remember to start the report by saying why it is being written (*in response to* ... or *at _____'s request*), and what ground it covers (*It describes the problems encountered ... and the measures taken to ...*).

ORGANIZING THE MATERIAL
Coldstream will probably begin by stating clearly and frankly the problems Hi-Flite has been experiencing in connection with the storage and delivery of goods:
   ... *up to 30 complaints a week* ...
   ... *a number of staff difficulties* ...
   ... *goods frequently damaged in transit* ...

Then, he will outline the causes. He may decide to present the facts schematically:
   (a) *Storage space is insufficient* ...
   (b) *Goods are often carelessly handled* ...
   (c) *Lorries often leave without* ...

Next, he will say what has been done so far to put matters right:
The following steps have been taken to remedy the situation:
   (a) ......
   (b) ......
   (c) ......
       etc.

ENDING THE REPORT: RECOMMENDATIONS
Assume you are writing the report about one month after Mr Wilkins (the customer) complained to Head Office. Say what effect your measures have had—e.g. on the number of customers' complaints each week. It is unlikely you will have solved all the problems within such a short time, and there will almost certainly be recommendations you want to make to Head Office on matters which only they can decide (e.g. to provide money for training of porters or drivers).

Alternative assignment

Suspecting that Kevin Landon and James Bascombe do not get on well together, Coldstream decides to get them both into his office at the same time and hear what they have to say about the problem of delivering furniture. Landon and Bascombe are both accustomed to speaking out, and the conversation becomes pretty lively though not very friendly. Write part or all of it as a dialogue among the three men.

HEARD OUTSIDE THE STOCK ROOM

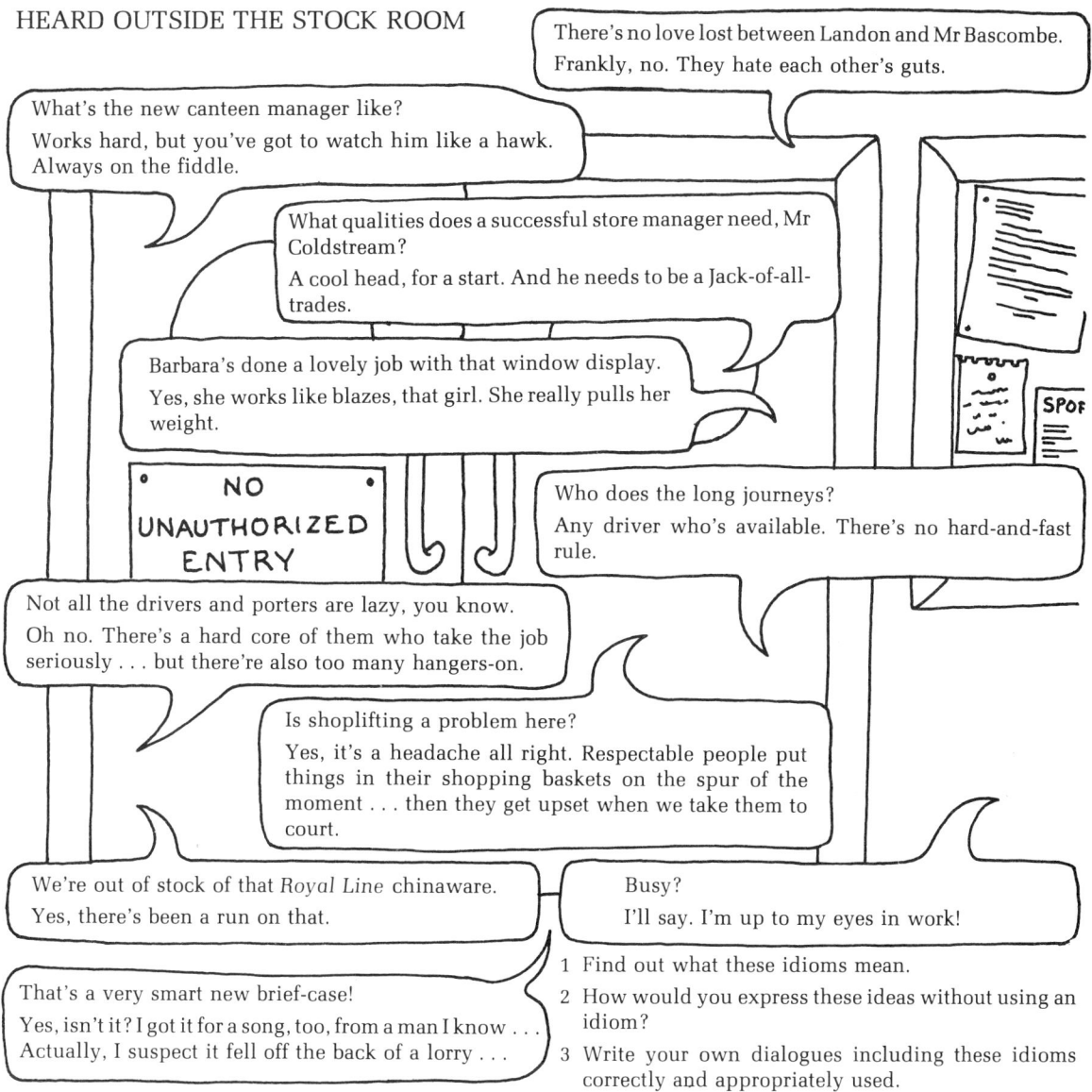

There's no love lost between Landon and Mr Bascombe.
Frankly, no. They hate each other's guts.

What's the new canteen manager like?
Works hard, but you've got to watch him like a hawk. Always on the fiddle.

What qualities does a successful store manager need, Mr Coldstream?
A cool head, for a start. And he needs to be a Jack-of-all-trades.

Barbara's done a lovely job with that window display.
Yes, she works like blazes, that girl. She really pulls her weight.

NO UNAUTHORIZED ENTRY

Who does the long journeys?
Any driver who's available. There's no hard-and-fast rule.

Not all the drivers and porters are lazy, you know.
Oh no. There's a hard core of them who take the job seriously . . . but there're also too many hangers-on.

Is shoplifting a problem here?
Yes, it's a headache all right. Respectable people put things in their shopping baskets on the spur of the moment . . . then they get upset when we take them to court.

We're out of stock of that *Royal Line* chinaware.
Yes, there's been a run on that.

Busy?
I'll say. I'm up to my eyes in work!

That's a very smart new brief-case!
Yes, isn't it? I got it for a song, too, from a man I know . . . Actually, I suspect it fell off the back of a lorry . . .

1 Find out what these idioms mean.
2 How would you express these ideas without using an idiom?
3 Write your own dialogues including these idioms correctly and appropriately used.

barnwood

UNDERSTANDING THE CASE

Read the case study in the Casebook and answer these questions.

1 Barnwood have been described as 'cautious but flexible' in their approach to exporting. Why? What makes them adopt this approach?
2 Explain briefly why toothpaste and laboratory glassware require different marketing methods.
3 What really persuaded Tom Price to make a sales trip to the Sultanate?
4 The newspaper article reprinted in the case study refers to the Sultanate's five-year plan. What is the plan's principal objective?
5 Which sentences in the article do you think made a particularly deep impression on Price?
6 As a result of the plan, the Sultanate will experience very rapid development. What sort of problems could this bring?
7 What has made Mrs Al Jabri President of a successful company? What is her ultimate ambition?
8 Why do you think Bannerman was made an honorary citizen of the Sultanate?
9 How much would Barnwood have to pay Mrs Al Jabri on annual sales of £50,000? Of £250,000? How much would they have to pay Bannerman if they achieved the same sales figures through him?
10 What does the Junior Assistant hope to gain from his acquaintanceship with Price?

VOCABULARY Overcoming the problems of affluence

Said Al Khalif, the Sultanate's Minister for Industry, is giving an informal press conference. Fill in the gaps in his remarks with words from the box.

Al Khalif . . . For an economy like ours, sudden economic _____ brings problems, but it also brings great _____. True, there's always the _____ of a s_____ in oil p_____ on the world market. That hasn't happened yet. Of course, a too rapid i_____ of w_____ can lead to _____. But so far we've avoided that.

   We're using our money to d_____ the i_____ of the country's e_____. We want to build up its essential s_____, so that when the oil runs out we shall have all the f_____ we need to survive as a fully _____ state.

   Meanwhile, we appreciate the a_____ of living in a very _____ society: the c_____ g_____ s in the shops, the _____ for education and travel, the s_____ that we enjoy among other oil-p_____ countries.

Our _____ t is good, so we can easily r_____ the c_____ we need for d_____ p_____ s, and we know we can s_____ these l_____ out of our future oil r_____.

boom	develop	industrialized
growth	raise	producing
inflation	service	prosperous
influx		
loan	amenity	consumer
price	capital	developing
revenue	credit	project
slump	development	purpose
wealth	economy	
	facility	
opportunity	goods	
possibility	infrastructure	
risk		
status		

62

A TACTICAL DISCUSSION—THE JUNIOR ASSISTANT AND MR PRICE

Read or listen to this dialogue.

The Junior Assistant to the Deputy Minister for Industry takes Mr Price to watch the Sultanate's football team in a practice game. He has something he wants to say to Mr Price in private.

Junior Assistant The difficulty with your shipment to Codorah has been overcome, I believe.

Price I'm bound to say that I find it incomprehensible that any difficulty should have arisen. All the documents were in order.

Junior Assistant I don't think you quite appreciate the way we do things here. You are, if I may say so, a stranger...

Price Thank you, but it's by no means my first trip to the Middle East—

Junior Assistant Precisely! That is why I feel it is my duty to point out these things to you now, and why I know you will understand. If you want to do business in this country, there are certain points you must bear in mind.

Price Well, yes, I'm sure you're right...

Junior Assistant For instance—you may not be aware of this, but it is my department which issues import licences. We can also revoke or cancel them. The regulations are liable to be amended at any time without notice.

Price You're saying, in other words, that it's advisable to keep on the right side of someone in the Ministry.

Junior Assistant I'll be frank with you. If you want to succeed here, you must know how to open doors. Otherwise, you can get into difficulties. I must warn you in the strongest possible terms: don't try to cut corners. It's not worth the risk.

Price H'mm. I can well believe it.

Junior Assistant I myself should be very pleased to help you. You know that family traditions are very strong in this country. I am connected with several of the families who are said to have founded our Sultanate many centuries ago.

Price Naturally I'll give your remarks careful consideration. Of course, I'm fully aware that I need advice and cooperation: an agent, a local manager, maybe even a business partner one day—I don't know yet. And then there's the question of bank guarantees, import documentation...

Junior Assistant No problem, I assure you. If I were you, Mr Price, I'd take care to get the right introductions to the right people—everything else will follow. But watch your step! You don't want to believe everything that other people tell you...

1. Listen again and find as many expressions as possible which are used to give someone advice or a warning, or to clarify a situation they may not understand.
2. Practise the expressions recorded after the dialogue on the tape.
3. With the following check-list to help you, do the role-playing exercise.

GIVING SOMEONE ADVICE OR A WARNING

I don't think you quite appreciate...
That's why I feel it's my duty to point out...
There are, if I may say so, certain points you must bear in mind.
You may not be aware of this, but...
In other words, it's advisable to...
I must warn you: don't try to...
It's not worth the risk.
If I were you, I would take care to...
Watch your step!
You don't want to...

Role-playing exercise

A packer/despatcher who works in the Barnwood factory has often been late for work during the last two months. Last week her Supervisor reported her for being drunk and incapable of carrying out her duties. Bill Hampson, the Personnel Manager, has called her to his office and intends to be tough with her. The Supervisor who reported her is also with him. When the packer arrives, she is accompanied by a shop steward—an elected representative of the workers in her section, who acts as the intermediary between the workers and the trade union. If the packer is sacked, her fellow workers may decide to stop work in protest.

DESK RESEARCH

Barnwood has been so successful as a manufacturer of laboratory glassware that it is now planning to diversify into other types of scientific equipment. It recently introduced a range of high-quality vacuum pumps, which are making a name for themselves in the home market and which Barnwood naturally hope to export.

The company's Marketing Director has selected the Middle East as one of his target areas, but he is not sure which country offers the most suitable market for Barnwood pumps. He wants to introduce the pumps into one, or possibly two, countries to begin with. He is seeking a market, or markets, with at least two of the following characteristics:

– size
– good growth prospects
– high value per unit sold.

So far, by collecting data from reports and publications, he has collected statistics concerning the sales of vacuum pumps in six Middle East countries. These figures refer to different types of equipment, from different manufacturers in Europe, America, Russia and the Far East. Nevertheless, he hopes that the figures give at least some indication of the market in each country.

IMPORTS OF VACUUM PUMPS						
Country	Value ($ 000)				No. of units sold	
	1987	1988	1989	1990	1989	1990
Bahrain	24	28	38	47	500	750
Iran	120	110	90	115	2000	2200
Iraq	92	99	89	87	1200	850
Jordan	14	12	19	37	200	450
Kuwait	149	167	184	190	2100	2100
Qatar	27	36	30	28	400	280

Consider the prospects these markets offer, and decide what advice you would give the Marketing Director. You will probably find it helpful to rank the six countries according to:

– size of market
– growth rate 1989–1990
– increase or decrease in number of units sold
– value per unit
– change in value per unit during the last twelve months.

THE RIGHT WORDS IN THE RIGHT PLACE

The consignment of glassware for Codorah arrived in the Sultanate on time but was (as we saw earlier) delayed by customs. Frank Bannerman became very worried, as he needed the goods urgently. He investigated, found out what was wrong, and then phoned Tom Price. Tom now has to send a telex to his Head Office, passing on the instructions that Frank has given him. This is what Frank said on the telephone:

Frank It's a nuisance, Tom, but the customs people are insisting on a consular invoice. They won't release the goods without it; there's just no way... Your guys will have to get it via the Sultanate's Embassy in London. They'll fill in the details there and stamp it. Don't forget to tell them to check that the Embassy seal is on it, otherwise it's not valid. Tell your office to airmail the invoice to us here as quick as they can...

There are some other points about this C.I. as well. Before they validate it, the Embassy may want to have it okayed by the London Chamber of Commerce, so you'd better make sure it goes there first, just to be on the safe side. Now, in the space marked *Consignee*, tell your boys to make sure the words *Frank Bannerman, Codorah* are written—not just *Codorah* ... And at the foot of the column marked *Price of merchandise*, see that they put the total in US dollars, with the sterling equivalent underneath ... Why? Because it's got to be done that way, that's why! One last thing—under *Quantity*, put *Cases*, not *Crates*, and under *Units* put *Pieces* not *Items* ... All right, so it sounds crazy, but I'm an old hand at this kind of thing and the right terminology saves time.

Now, tell your office to move like greased lightning. I expect the Embassy will close early on Friday for midday prayers; if they don't get the invoice fixed before the weekend, then we're really up the creek. Get that telex off right away, Tom. Don't worry. You'll get priority. I've already had a word with the telex operator at your hotel!

Draft Price's telex for him. (For notes about writing telex messages, see Appendix, Section 3.)

WRITTEN ASSIGNMENT

When Tom Price returns from a business trip, he usually writes a short report about it and circulates copies to his senior executives. He bases his reports mainly on the information contained in his diary or notebook.

Imagine you are Tom Price. Write the report he would make following his visit to the Sultanate.

LAYOUT AND TITLE

This report will almost certainly be in the form of a memo. It will be quite formal, and as brief as possible. If you show the layout in full, you can start like this:

From Managing Director
To   List A
Date ...

List A contains the names of a group of people or departments to whom documents are routinely circulated. In a large organization, the use of these circulation or distribution lists saves continual re-typing of columns of names.

The title will probably be as follows: *Report on my trip to the Sultanate 5–12 June* or simply *Visit to the Sultanate 5–12 June*.

Make sure you organize your information carefully and present it in the form of paragraphs. Good paragraphing is as important as good grammar if the report is to be easy to read and understand. Paragraphs in reports are often numbered, and given headings; this makes it easier for the writer to think clearly, and easier for the reader to see at a glance what the report contains.

PRESENTING YOUR MATERIAL

Here is a possible structure for Tom Price's report. Use this format if you wish or devise one of your own.

1 *Introduction*: say why you went to the Sultanate, and what you hoped to achieve.

2 *The background*: very briefly, give one or two important facts about the Sultanate. You could mention, for example, its population, its Gross National Product or oil revenues for the last twelve months; perhaps give a word or two about its form of government.

3 *The market*: give figures (in this case, you will invent some) for imports of laboratory equipment, and for expenditure on education, scientific research or industrial development. The future is more important than the past: mention the five-year plan, or any other project which is significant. Lengthy statistical tables, however, will appear in appendices, not in the report itself. All you need to do is refer to them, e.g. *according to estimates published by the Ministry of Industry (see Appendix A)*.

4 *Meetings and contacts*: summarize the main points from Price's notebook. You may find it easier and neater to lay these out as a series of sub-paragraphs:
   4.1 *Mrs Khalifa Al Jabri* ...
   4.2 *Mr Frank Bannerman* ...
      etc.

5 *Recommendations*: say briefly why you think Barnwood should, or should not, try to enter this new market. Assuming that you think it should try, say what steps the company should take. Again, you may find it helpful to list your recommendations as numbered sub-paragraphs:
   ... therefore make the following recommendations:
   5.1 *that Barnwood should* ...
   5.2 *that enquiries should be made* ...
   5.3 *that our company should try to persuade* ...
Remember that in any list, all the items must have the same grammatical structure.

Alternative assignment

In the Casebook, you were asked to consider the means Barnwood should use to break into the market for laboratory glassware in the Sultanate. Your group has now discussed the problem and has reached its conclusions. In about 100–150 words, summarize the different views that were expressed and say what was finally decided.

HEARD IN THE AIRPORT LOUNGE

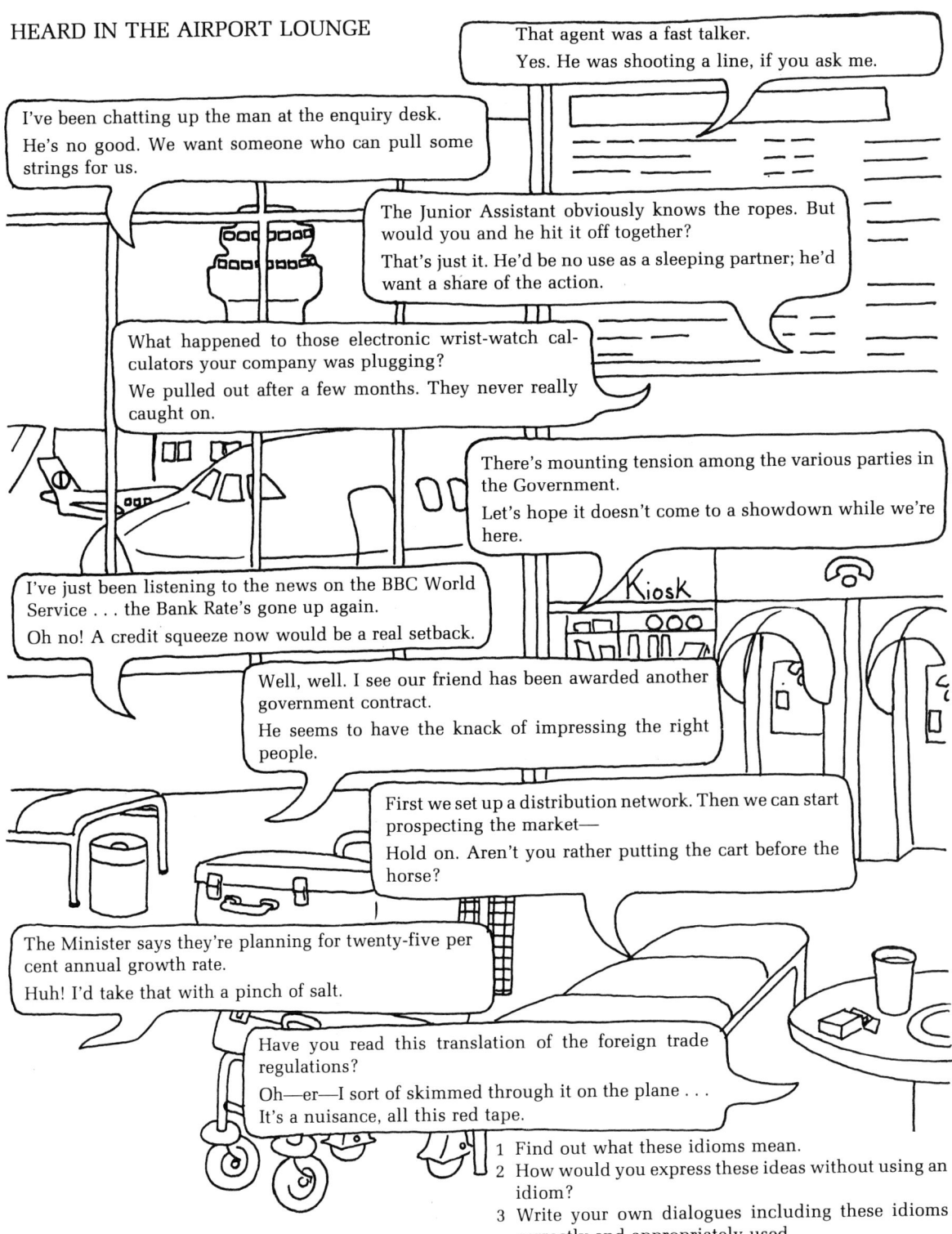

That agent was a fast talker.
Yes. He was shooting a line, if you ask me.

I've been chatting up the man at the enquiry desk.
He's no good. We want someone who can pull some strings for us.

The Junior Assistant obviously knows the ropes. But would you and he hit it off together?
That's just it. He'd be no use as a sleeping partner; he'd want a share of the action.

What happened to those electronic wrist-watch calculators your company was plugging?
We pulled out after a few months. They never really caught on.

There's mounting tension among the various parties in the Government.
Let's hope it doesn't come to a showdown while we're here.

I've just been listening to the news on the BBC World Service... the Bank Rate's gone up again.
Oh no! A credit squeeze now would be a real setback.

Well, well. I see our friend has been awarded another government contract.
He seems to have the knack of impressing the right people.

First we set up a distribution network. Then we can start prospecting the market—
Hold on. Aren't you rather putting the cart before the horse?

The Minister says they're planning for twenty-five per cent annual growth rate.
Huh! I'd take that with a pinch of salt.

Have you read this translation of the foreign trade regulations?
Oh—er—I sort of skimmed through it on the plane...
It's a nuisance, all this red tape.

1 Find out what these idioms mean.
2 How would you express these ideas without using an idiom?
3 Write your own dialogues including these idioms correctly and appropriately used.

EASY-GO

UNDERSTANDING THE CASE
Read the case study in the Casebook and answer these questions.

1 Why did Easy Go send William Merton to Malaysia?
2 How did Merton explain his conduct to the court?
3 Why do you think Merton was given a suspended sentence?
4 How does this affect the case?
5 What evidence is there that the General Manager is a fair person?
6 What purpose does the General Manager have in 'playing down the incident'?
7 In what way does the Head of Overseas Sales hint that the company is partly to blame for Merton's present troubles?
8 If you were Head of Overseas Sales, how would you interpret Bill Merton's letter? What does it reveal?
9 In the discussion between Jason Porter and Bob Pickup, several possible causes are mentioned for Merton's breakdown. What are they?
10 How does Bill Merton feel about Easy Go's franchising operation in Malaysia?

VOCABULARY The men who sell Easy Go

Bill Merton is talking, rather late at night, to some men he has met in a hotel. Fill in the gaps in his remarks from the box below, in the usual way.

Merton . . . You see, my job in Malaysia is to set up a f____ n__w__ for Easy Go outboards. Each _____ will be an independent trader. He'll be in b_____ on his own a_____, so he'll really have a s_____ in the company's success.

He'll be p_____ our products with our help. In return, he won't _____ any other make of outboard motor. It's an ex____ agreement.

Naturally, I won't take just anybody. I've got to have dealers who are financially _____. And there are personal qu____. R____, i____, good business _____: that's what I look for.

We demand a capital _____ on their p_____, too. They can pay it all at once in a l_____ s_____, or by _____s, so much a month, out of i_____. That's an added incentive to make profits! They can f_____ their own prices, so they really s_____ to make a great _____ if they work hard.

But profits won't be i_____, I can tell you. It will take a year or two for Easy Go to become _____ in the Malaysian market. That's why we insist on a three-year agreement _____ly. It protects us as well as them.

business	exclusive(ly)	account
deal	immediate(ly)	income
franchise	initial(ly)	instalment
franchisee	instant(ly)	lump
investment	sound(ly)	network
part		stake
	initiative	sum
establish	quality	
fix	reliability	
handle	sense	
insist		
promote		
stand		

67

AN UNEXPECTED VISITOR

Read or listen to the dialogue.

Bob Pickup is sitting in his office one afternoon when his secretary announces an unexpected visitor—Bill Merton's wife, Belinda.

Bob Hullo, Belinda. This is a surprise. I thought you were still in Hong Kong. Have a chair.

Belinda Thank you. I came back from Hong Kong because—well, because I'm very anxious about Bill. I wanted to talk to my family about it and to ask your advice.

Bob We're all anxious about Bill. But he isn't here, he's in Singapore. Tomorrow he's flying to Malacca. In fact, he's expecting you to join him.

Belinda Yes, I know, but if I do, do you think he'll be pleased to see me?

Bob I should have thought he would be, yes.

Belinda I wish I thought so too.

Bob I had a letter from him the other day. He's very anxious that you should go back to him.

Belinda Oh, he says that, I daresay. He'd rather I was with him so he could keep his eye on me.

Bob He'd prefer to have his wife with him rather than pick up her accounts in every department store in the Far East, yes! . . . OK, I shouldn't have said that. But—

Belinda Suppose I were to fly to Malacca tomorrow, do you think it would help?

Bob It might. It depends, really. I mean, it would depend on why you did it.

Belinda I don't suppose he'll be staying in Malacca for long, will he?

Bob Well—that rather depends on how things turn out . . .

Belinda It's a charming little town, of course, but not very exciting.

Bob I shouldn't wonder if you stirred it up a bit.

Belinda . . . All right then! Maybe I will go, after all . . . If only he wouldn't sleep with a Dictaphone under his pillow! No, never mind. I'll do it. There's just one problem—

Bob I had a feeling there might be.

Belinda I'm absolutely flat broke. I practically had to hitchhike back to Sydney from Hong Kong. You know I'd sooner die than ask you for money, Bob . . . but if you could help me to get back to Malacca, perhaps I could help Bill to sort things out . . .

1 Listen again and find as many expressions as possible which are used to talk about imaginary time—ways of saying what you wish, what you would prefer, or what you guess might be possible.

2 Practise the expressions recorded after the dialogue on the tape.

3 With the following check-list to help you, do the role-playing exercise.

WISHING, PREFERRING AND GUESSING

if I . . ., do you think he will . . .?

I should have thought he would . . .

I wish there was . . .

I'd rather he didn't . . .

Suppose I were to . . ., do you think it would . . .?

It would depend on why . . .

If only he wouldn't . . .

I'd sooner . . . than . . .

Role-playing exercise

Tun Abdul Kadir owns a small but prosperous boatyard and yacht chandlery on the Malacca waterfront. His son, Saleh, is twenty years old and Kadir wants him to start work in the boat business as an Easy Go franchisee. Saleh, however, is a gifted musician and mathematician and wants to study abroad. One evening, he and his father are drinking coffee on the verandah of the Ocean Front Hotel when they see Bill Merton (whom they know quite well) and another acquaintance of theirs from the office of the British International Advisory Council in Kuala Lumpur. Soon, all of them are discussing the possible futures that are open to Saleh.

CLAIMING EXPENSES

Michael Stell is a sales representative for Easy Go's Agricultural Division. He travels widely and is away from Head Office for long periods. On these trips he incurs all kinds of expenses, some of which he pays in cash, some with his personal credit card, some with a company credit card. At the end of the month he sends his firm's Finance Officer a statement of all these outgoings, and in due course receives a cheque by way of reimbursement for money which he has spent out of his own pocket.

Part of Michael's statement for October 1991 is shown below. As you can see, the claim form was designed in days when the firm's representatives did relatively little travelling; it is quite inadequate for today's needs, and the Finance Officer has at last made up his mind to design a new and better form.

Study Michael Stell's claim, consider all the different sorts of expense that such a form needs to show, and draft a new one for the Finance Officer.

EASY GO   Sheet 1 of 4 sheets

Statement of expenses incurred   Date .. Oct ..... 19 .91...

Date	Description	$
1.10	Petrol (credit card voucher attached)	20.73
	Aurora Motel, Bathurst (receipt attached; personal cheque)	58.95
4.10	Car broke down. Towing and repairs (company credit card)	76.20
5.10	Lunch with customer (Grapho Bearings) — cash.	36.50
	Hire of car for 3 days, including insurance + mileage charges (own credit card)	146.90
	Hotel Derby, Goulburn, 3 days. (personal cheque)	186.21
6.10	Stationery + postage stamps	6.50
7.10	Dinner with customer and wife — inc. drinks, tickets, etc. (Part cash, part credit card. Documents attached, where available)	206.80
8.10	Petrol etc. for hired car	47.50
	Petrol for own car (invoice total: 29.65) Weekend at Shellharbour — deduct 15.00)	14.65
11.10	Telephone bill (total 120.94; ⅓ allowable for business)	40.31
	TOTAL CARRIED FORWARD	841.25

Name M. J. Stell   Department Agri. Division
Post Sales Representative   Signature M Stell

THE RIGHT WORDS IN THE RIGHT PLACE

At Easy Go, all junior and middle managers' records are periodically reviewed by a meeting of department heads. A few months ago, Bill Merton was considered for promotion. The Personnel Manager, who has a high opinion of Merton, briefly summarized the facts about his career as he saw them. Then the Development Manager did the same. He dislikes Merton intensely: a simple case of personality clash.

Below, you can see Merton's Personal Record Form, and the opening words of the two managers' remarks. Write the rest of what they said, selecting and presenting the facts to give first a good impression of Merton, then a bad one.

EASY GO PERSONAL RECORD SHEET

1 **FULL NAME** William Allardyce MERTON   MR/~~MRS~~/~~MISS~~

   DATE OF BIRTH 15 September 1954   **PLACE OF BIRTH** Derby, England

   NATIONALITY AT BIRTH British   **NATIONALITY NOW** Australian (from 25 March 1988)

   MARITAL STATUS Married (August 1987)   **CHILDREN** None
   Belinda (nee Heseltine)

2 **EDUCATION**
   Give schools, colleges, etc. with dates, qualifications, etc.

   1969-74 St Egbert's Secondary Modern School, Derby
   1976-78 Derby College of Higher Education: obtained Higher National Diploma in Business Studies

3 **PREVIOUS WORK EXPERIENCE**
   Give all previous employers with addresses, dates, particulars of positions held and final salary.

   1974-76 Various unskilled jobs: dishwasher, ice-cream vendor, nightclub attendant, etc.
   1978-82 Elite Footwear Co. Ltd, Kendal, England: Sales Representative, Northeast England — promoted
            to Assistant Sales Manager, 1981. Salary approximately £7,600 plus car, etc.
   1982-85 Merton Marketing Consultants: partner. Resigned after 10 months to emigrate.

4 **INTERESTS/HOBBIES**
   Mention any specialist qualifications, membership of professional bodies, etc.

   Small-boat sailing (R.Y.A. Yachtmaster's Certificate I and II); Southeast Asian language and culture –
   especially Thai/Japanese shadow plays; photography; Zen Buddhism.

FOR OFFICIAL USE ONLY

5 Joined Easy Go: 20 November 1983 (Agricultural Division)
   Post: Overseas Sales Representative (Southeast Asia)

   1984-85 Singapore: established new branch office.
   1985-86 Bangkok: took over from Dixon as acting Area Manager.
   1986   Confirmed as Area Manager, Thailand.
            Completed Thai language course – intermediate.
   1987   Assistant Regional Sales Manager (Southeast Asia)
            Passed Malaysian language course – advanced.
            Attended International Marketing Seminar (Vancouver).
   1988   Regional Sales Manager (located Sydney, pending transfer to Singapore)
   1989   Seconded to Marine Division to set up distribution network in Malaysia.

Personnel Manager There's no doubt whatever in my mind that we've got a first-rate man here. He's mature, still young . . .

Development Manager Well, I'm not sure I can go along with you. If we look at this man's career in a little more detail, we find that he left school at the first possible moment, . . .

WRITTEN ASSIGNMENT

The Chairman of Easy Go is Sir Humphrey Duckworth, a former Australian rugby international and MP, who now spends most of his time in the Bahamas. Jason Porter is disgruntled one morning to receive a cable from Sir Humphrey, saying that he has read newspaper reports of Merton's escapade in Malaya ('How the hell did the news reach Nassau?' Porter asks Bob Pickup). The cable goes on: WHO IS THIS MERTON PLEASE SEND FULL REPORT OF CIRCUMSTANCES AND ACTION TAKEN DUCKWORTH.

> Draft Jason Porter's report to Sir Humphrey. Do not give details of the incident in Kuantan—a copy of Merton's report will be attached as an appendix—but tell Sir Humphrey everything you know about Merton's background and problems, and reassure him that the good name and interests of Easy Go are being safeguarded.

SATISFYING SIR HUMPHREY

This report is best presented in the form of a letter, marked *Personal and Confidential*. It is unlikely to lead to any further action, provided you write it well. Begin it *Dear Sir Humphrey* and end *Yours sincerely, Jason Porter, General Manager*.

THE BODY OF THE REPORT

There are no *Procedures* here, because you are simply telling the Chairman what you already know. (Use all the information you can find in the Workbook as well as the Casebook.) The first paragraph of your letter, however, —the *Terms of reference*—ought to give Sir Humphrey some reassurance:

I appreciate your concern . . .

Your anxiety is very natural . . .

It is understandable that you should want to know . . .

Please be assured, however, that the matter is well in hand . . .

I can assure you/You may rest assured, however, that we are taking the necessary steps . . .

WHO IS THIS MERTON?

Outline Merton's background very briefly. The type of education he received may be worth mentioning, but the actual name of the school he attended is not. Give somewhat fuller details of his career with Easy Go. There is no need to copy every little piece of information from his Personal Record Form, but make it clear that Merton has an impressive track record, is a good linguist, and has a variety of interests and accomplishments.

Then deal with his personal problems, insofar as you know and understand them:

His chief difficulty, as I understand it, is that . . .

It appears, however, that he has recently been under severe strain owing to . . .

The root of Merton's present troubles, as far as I can make out, is . . .

It is most unfortunate that Merton should have . . .

Be very careful not to make any statement of fact about the Mertons that you do not know to be true. Remember, at the same time, that you must justify to Sir Humphrey Merton's rapid promotion in the company and the responsibility that he has been entrusted with.

ACTION TAKEN

This will have been decided at the group discussion of the case. (Alternatively, make your own decision.) Explain the reason for the decision very briefly; if you have confidence in your own judgement, you do not foresee any possible mistake and therefore do not need to make excuses in advance.

End the letter with a sentence or two offering to send further information if required and promising to keep Sir Humphrey informed about any further developments.

Alternative assignment

Acting for Bob Pickup, draft a cable to be sent to Bill Merton at the Ocean Front Hotel, Malacca. Remember that he may be in an excitable or a depressed state of mind, and that Belinda may or may not be with him. The cable should inform him of the decision that has been made about his immediate future. Alternatively, it may simply recall him to Head Office—but this should only be done as a last resort.

HEARD IN THE FOYER OF SYDNEY OPERA HOUSE

Merton's reckoned to be a high flier, isn't he?
He's in the running for the top marketing job, when the present man goes.

She doesn't like her new job much.
A square peg in a round hole, as they say.

What did you make of his letter? It seemed pretty level-headed to me.
Yes, but reading between the lines, I thought I could detect signs of strain.

The wine waiter tried to short-change you, did he?
Yes, so I gave him a piece of my mind.

I'd love to take a parcel to Jakarta for you, Bob . . . Only thing is, I'm overweight already on my air luggage.
Don't worry, you won't be out of pocket. If you have to pay any excess, just let me know.

So I said to her, 'You can't just go on running up bills and expect me to pay them.'
That's the stuff! What did she do?
She walked out on me.

I think we're going to end up giving this man his sick leave, just as he asks.
Maybe. But it goes against the grain.

Who in Malaysia buys outboard motors anyway?
There's a sizeable leisure market. But a lot of fishermen have taken to using outboards—if we can get a foot in the door there, we'll be laughing.

How do you like working for that firm?
They're marvellous. They've just given me a loan to buy a house: low rate of interest, no strings attached!

His work's gone off lately. I think he needs a holiday.
That's what comes of burning the candle at both ends.

1. Find out what these idioms mean.
2. How would you express these ideas without using an idiom?
3. Write your own dialogues including these idioms correctly and appropriately used.

MACQUILTER

UNDERSTANDING THE CASE

Read the case study in the Casebook and answer these questions.

1. What special problems face a company like Macquilter in selling golf equipment overseas?
2. How might golfers learn about Macquilter products?
3. Why is Young so determined to improve sales in Japan?
4. Can you suggest any reasons why Macquilter has so far not done very well in Japan?
5. Why does Young believe that Kato is the best man to sell Macquilter products there?
6. What has Kato come to Canada to do?
7. What thoughts are probably passing through Kato's mind as he walks onto the 18th green?
8. When Young, Boyers and Weiss discuss the problem of developing the Japanese market, each argues strongly in favour of his own proposals. What personal or professional reasons might make them do this?
9. Why does Kakimoto want 'a fixed-price contract, negotiable each year'?
10. What are the main features of a franchise operation?

VOCABULARY An up-market game

Frank Boyers is talking to a young Product Executive who has just joined the firm. It is an informal chat, as they drive along the freeway to the office. Fill in the gaps in Frank's remarks from the box below.

Boyers We haven't yet discovered how to achieve satisfactory m_____ p_____ in Japan. We have complete c_____ in our p_____ r_____, and we know that there's a growing d_____ over there for h_____-_____ golf e_____.
   Only the other day, a leading s_____ g_____ manufacturer in Tokyo a_____ us with a p_____ to make Macquilter products under _____. He said he wanted to market a p_____ range; that's what he called it. We weren't able to r_____ a_____ with him because we couldn't get any _____ that his stuff would be up to _____. We can't afford to have our name associated with anything that looks _____.
   Golfers are very f_____-conscious. They want gear that's s_____ as well as being well made. For businessmen, especially, it's a _____ pastime that can enhance an executive's _____.
   One customer of ours wanted a really _____ set of clubs: gold-plated shafts, no less! The way he hit the ball wasn't quite so _____, though.

demand	cheap	agreement
equipment	de luxe	assurance
goods	exclusive	confidence
market	fashion	guarantee
penetration	high	licence
product	impressive	proposal
range	low	
	luxury	sport
grade	popular	sporting
prestige	stylish	sports
quality		
standard	approach	
status	reach	

ANOTHER GAME OF GOLF

Read or listen to the dialogue.
Hiroshi Kato and Ursula Young, Herbie's wife, are having an early morning round of golf before Hiroshi flies back to Tokyo.

Ursula You're very thoughtful today, Hiroshi. What's up?

Kato Oh—nothing. It's not important.

Ursula Come on! What's on your mind?

Kato Well, I'm thinking of all the promises I've made to Macquilters. Sometimes I wonder if I've bitten off more than I can chew.

Ursula Now look. You've no need to worry. There's no commitment on either side at this stage. And I'm sure, if they do decide to give you the dealership in Japan, it'll be because they have complete faith in you.

Kato It would be a mark of confidence, yes. It's just that sometimes I get cold feet. But don't let it worry you. I'm sure everything will be all right.

Ursula If anyone can penetrate the Japanese market, Hiroshi, I'm sure you can. I just wonder whether our designs are right . . .

Kato I'm convinced they are. Look at all the prize-money I've won with Macquilter products!

Ursula Yes, you haven't done too badly.

Kato There you are, then. If it's any encouragement to you, one of my strongest rivals has started using Macquilter clubs because he knows I use them.

Ursula H'mm. That's reassuring, I suppose. You'd better make sure you beat him, next time round!

Kato Ah—the golfing journalists seem to be a bit doubtful.

Ursula Oh, you don't want to take any notice of them . . .

1 Listen again and find as many expressions as possible which are used to give reassurance or encouragement.

2 Practise the expressions recorded after the dialogue on the tape.

3 With the following check-list to help you, do the role-playing exercise.

REASSURING AND ENCOURAGING

You've no need to worry/feel anxious.

I'm sure . . .

Look at . . .!

There you are then; I told you so.

It's not worth ——ing . . .

After all, you did . . .

I don't think it's . . .

I daresay it isn't as bad as you think/all that.

You don't want to take any notice of . . .

Role-playing exercise

Peter, Kay and Tony are having a cup of coffee in the works canteen. Kay is nervous; she's taking her driving test tomorrow. She is convinced the examiner will be rude, and she is worried about: reversing; emergency stopping; driving in heavy traffic; starting the car on a steep hill; questions about traffic regulations. The others, who have passed their tests, reassure her on all these points.

CAN HE DO IT?

On Sunday, 8 November, Frank Boyers will fly into Tokyo at 1800 hours local time. He will fly out again on Thursday, 12 November at 1930 hours. Between those two times he has a lot of ground to cover. Here are the appointments he has made and the things he wants to do:

> **Tokyo**   Fixed appointment for 10 November at 7 p.m. Likely to end up in night club – no sleep!
>
> Must spend at least 3 hours sometime at Trade Fair – open every day 11 a.m. to midnight, from 11 November.
>
> At least 8 hours for other visits, between 8 a.m. and 6 p.m., any day.
>
> **Sapporo**   Several visits: One pencilled in for 2 p.m. on 9 November. Day's skiing, if at all possible.
>
> **Osaka**   Must meet agent, who leaves early on 11 November. Vital meeting scheduled for 11.30 a.m. on 12 November.
>
> **Fukuoka**   Several good friends to visit – overnight stay if possible. Hoping to finalize important contract with supplier: take him to dinner.

Make out an itinerary for Boyers. He intends to travel by air. The timetables are shown below. Remember that he needs up to 2 hours for the journey between the airport and the city centre, and must report for his flight at least half an hour before take-off.

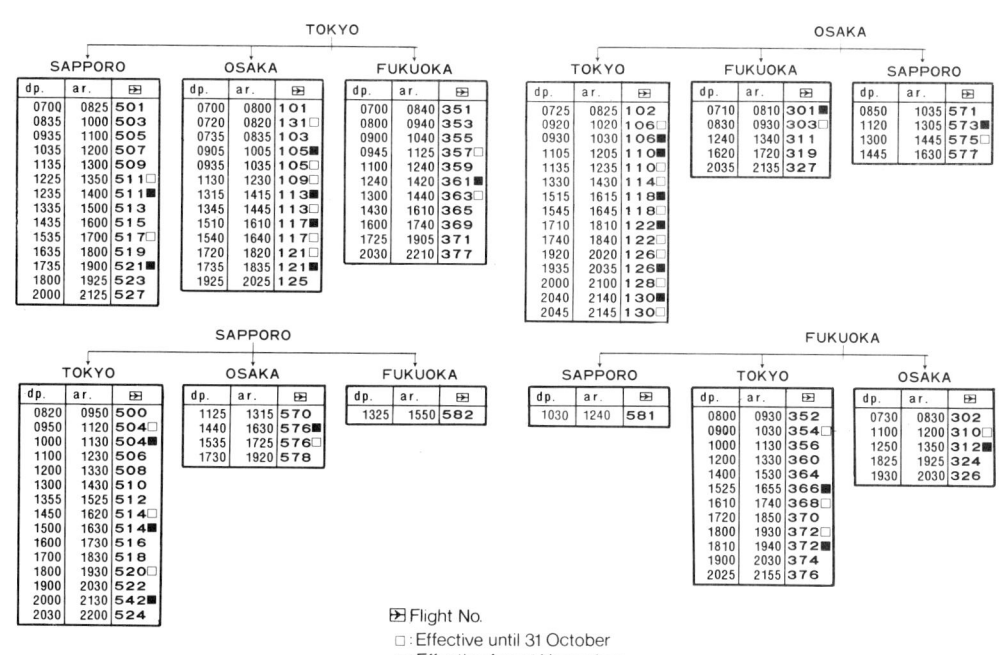

⊞ Flight No.
□ : Effective until 31 October
■ : Effective from 1 November

THE RIGHT WORDS IN THE RIGHT PLACE

A few months ago, Frank Boyers was in Tokyo and had dinner one evening in a restaurant with Toshi Kakimoto. After the meal, Kakimoto pulled out an impressive-looking document and passed it across to Boyers. 'This is the Annual Report for my group of companies,' he said. 'A lot of our shareholders aren't Japanese, and I need a summary of some of the main points in English. If I tell you more or less what these points are, do you think you could put them into good formal English for me?' Boyers agreed to do his best.

> Below are five points that Kakimoto made, based on his Annual Report. The first one is also shown as Frank Boyers expressed it. Rewrite the other four in the same style.

Example

Kakimoto Well, to start with, the Report says that things have been going much better since we got over that bad patch a couple of years ago.

There has been a marked recovery in the group's fortunes over the past two years.

1 Then it says that our retail shops have done especially well—they made forty million yen before tax!

2 Any branch whose performance doesn't match up to the rest, we get rid of, I can tell you. But we're still interested in buying new shops if we think they're worth putting money into.

3 We've done pretty well on the clothing side, too. Sales are going up all the time. We've been pushing them really hard overseas—it's been a terrific year for exports.

4 By the way, we're branching out a bit. We've started selling synthetic foods—quite successful, believe it or not.

WRITTEN ASSIGNMENT

Herbie Young recently met a South Korean businessman called Kim. Mr Kim convinced him that Macquilter could do good business in South Korea, and after discussing the matter Herbie agreed to let Kim act as the Macquilter agent in that area. Kim returned to Seoul and sent Herbie a letter confirming the points they had settled. Unfortunately, some of Kim's points were not quite what Herbie had intended, and one important point had been left out altogether. This is what part of Kim's letter looked like after Herbie had written his own notes on it.

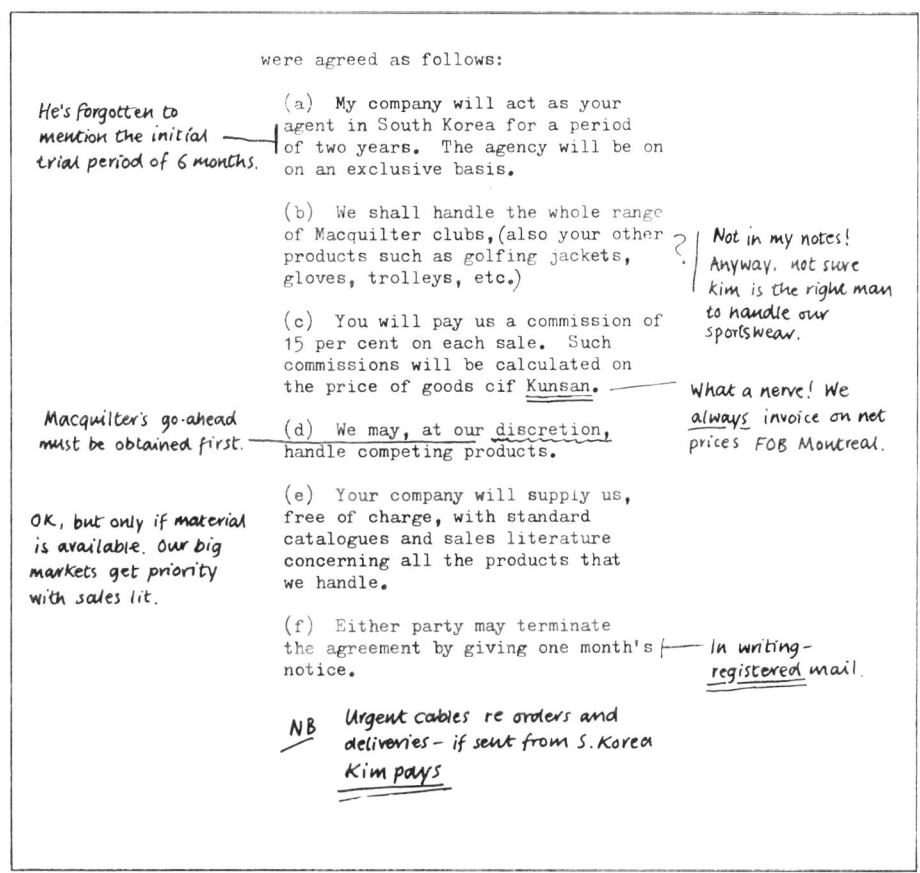

Write to Mr Kim, pointing out and correcting the inaccuracies in his letter. Be firm, but polite.

Alternative assignment

Frank Boyers, Head of Marketing, believes that Macquilter should move into other sports as well as golf. Tennis is his first choice, and he wants his firm to make a range of good-quality tennis rackets. Export markets will be vital. Before commissioning in-depth studies from marketing consultants, however, he decides to collect as many informal reports as he can from people in his department who have first-hand knowledge of various countries.

You joined the staff of his department a short time ago. He has asked you to write a short report for him, giving him as much information as you possess about tennis as it is played in your country. How popular is it? Who plays it? Where do players get their equipment? Is it expensive? Do you know of any factors which would help or hinder promotion of Macquilter tennis rackets? Have you any specific suggestions or recommendations to make, based on your own knowledge of the country?

77

HEARD IN THE LOCKER ROOM

Done any research yet into possible manufacturers?
Well, I've sounded out a number of firms, and the response is encouraging.

Hiroshi told me he was thinking of taking up flower arranging—I ask you!
If he does, you can bet your bottom dollar he'll work at it till he's number one in Japan.

Hey, I like your tie: the Hole-in-One Club, eh?
That's right. Actually, I don't care for the tie, but it does put you one up on your opponents.

My little daughter's a natural ice-skater. She's thirteen, and already she's training for the next Olympics.
I'm not surprised. In ice-skating, you're over the hill at a very early age.

How are your plans for a radio-controlled lawn mower coming along?
Not too good. The prototype smashed through the neighbour's fence, so it's back to square one.

I don't know how it is. I thought I had the soundest portfolio of securities this side of the Rocky Mountains—and yet . . .
Don't say you're losing your touch!

How's the tournament going?
Oh Geoffrey's way ahead. If you ask me, it's all over, bar the shouting.

What do you reckon the market potential for your products is in the Far East?
Oh boy—if we can just get it right—the sky's the limit!

They've invested a lot of money in their sales effort.
Yes, they're determined to go for broke. But if they do hit the jackpot, the shares will rocket. So get in on the ground floor!

Who will get the dealership, do you think?
Need you ask? It's a foregone conclusion!

1 Find out what these idioms mean.
2 How would you express these ideas without using an idiom?
3 Write your own dialogues including these idioms correctly and appropriately used.

WESTMEATH

UNDERSTANDING THE CASE
Read the case study in the Casebook and answer these questions.
1. What is the attitude of the Government of the Republic of Ireland towards foreign investment?
2. Why did Karlstad-Poly not announce plans for large-scale automation at the time they took over Westmeath?
3. What do the twenty unofficial strikers at Westmeath hope to gain by their action?
4. If there are to be redundancies at Westmeath, who will have to decide their timing and extent?
5. Which groups of workers will be hardest hit by the introduction of automation?
6. Which group of workers would be likely to put up the most effective resistance?
7. Do Karlstad-Poly and the Westmeath management have the same targets for the company?
8. How can the different parties in this conflict (that is: Westmeath management, Westmeath workers, and Karlstad-Poly) communicate with each other?
9. Are the means of communication that they use likely to affect the actions or decisions of the different parties?
10. What can the employer do to make automation more acceptable to the workforce?

VOCABULARY Two points of view

A Westmeath worker and the Factory Manager are arguing about the changes that are promised—or threatened—in their company. Fill in the gaps in their remarks from the box below.

Worker We know that nowadays almost any industrial p_____ can be c_____ by some sort of m_____. The h_____ has become very s_____, and it's _____ cheap. I mean, it's cheap c_____ with the cost of l_____. A lot of the w_____ in this factory are frightened of r_____. People are being l_____ o_____ already in some firms.

Manager Look, it's no good trying to put the clock back. My job's at risk too, you know. You can't stop _____. You've got to realize that a p_____ company like this one depends on i_____ and new t_____.

Worker Sure, we've said we're willing to accept partial a_____, but only if it's p_____ _____ over several years. We've got to have time to _____ to it.

Manager It's not practical to i_____ such a _____ control t_____ bit by bit. You can't do a thing like this p_____. It's got to be a single o_____; at one fell swoop, as they say.

Worker Well, we on the shop floor think a crash p_____ like that is a serious threat to the company. High-technology c_____ s_____ should be _____ gradually.

Manager Come off it, Paddy. I can understand that some less skilled _____s are afraid of being _____ by the computer. But a machine is no _____ for a highly trained and experienced o_____. And don't forget all the new jobs that are going to be created! A d_____-_____ s_____ is only as good as its s_____: the programmes that control it.

Worker And may I ask who's going to control the _____ers?

innovation	advanced	adjust
introduction	piecemeal	control
operation	progressive	introduce
process	sophisticated	lay off
processing		phase in
progress	employee	replace
	labour	substitute
automation	operative	
data	programmer	compared
hardware	worker	relatively
microcircuit		redundant
programme		redundancy
software		
system		
technique		
technology		

SHOP-FLOOR WORKER JOINS THE BOARD

Read or listen to the dialogue.

Paddy O'Reilly, Westmeath's recently elected worker-director, is being interviewed by a journalist, Kate Mulligan.

Mulligan Tell me, Paddy, how did you feel when they first made you a worker-director? A bit apprehensive?

O'Reilly That's putting it mildly. I was scared out of my wits. You see, I've been a working man all my life—I joined the company as an apprentice when I left school—and I'm also a union man through and through. I was a shop steward for over ten years, but ... serving on the Board, well, that's a different kettle of fish altogether.

Mulligan How do you mean? Did you think the other members would give you the cold shoulder or something? Laugh at you behind your back?

O'Reilly Heavens, no! I wasn't worried about that. What I'm trying to say is, I was expecting to be completely out of my depth. I thought I would be asked my opinion about financial reports, profit and loss accounts, cash flows, that sort of thing ...

Mulligan Ah, you felt you wouldn't be able to hold your own in that sort of discussion.

O'Reilly Well, let's put it this way, I haven't got much of an education—I mean I haven't got a degree or diplomas of any kind—I certainly haven't been to business school like some of the directors, so ... to be honest, I was afraid of making a damn fool of myself.

Mulligan I'm not surprised. I think most of us would have felt like that if we'd been in your shoes. Anyway, how did things work out?

O'Reilly Not bad at all. Actually, the Board members have bent over backwards to be nice to me—it's rather embarrassing really. And if there's any item on the agenda which affects the workers—the shop floor—then I'm usually the first to be asked to give my opinion.

Mulligan Can you give me an example?

O'Reilly Oh, anything to do with pay or working conditions; production methods; safety; workers' grievances ...

Mulligan And what happens when they start talking about balance sheets?

O'Reilly Ha! usually the Company Secretary or the Financial Director is so eager to do the talking that no one else can get a word in edgeways!

Mulligan I don't doubt that. So, in other words, you're happy about the contribution you've made to discussions?

O'Reilly Yes, I am, and if all these rumours about introducing robots turn out to be true, the members of the Board will be hearing a good deal more from me in the future ...

1 Listen again and find as many expressions as possible which are used to clarify what someone has said.

2 Practise the expressions recorded after the dialogue on the tape.

3 With the following check-list to help you, do the role-playing exercise.

EXPLAINING, CONFIRMING AND CLARIFYING

That's putting it mildly! I was ...
You see, ...
What I'm trying to say is ...
Well, let's put it this way, ...
I mean, ...
Actually, ...
So, in other words, ...

Role-playing exercise

Two of Westmeath's senior managers think the company needs more information about the products and marketing strategies of rival companies. It would be very useful if management knew in advance what price changes their competitors were planning, what new products they had in the pipeline, or what technical and design modifications they had up their sleeves.

To help them gather this type of sensitive data, the two men wish to appoint a market intelligence executive. This person would monitor the operations of other kitchen equipment manufacturers, collecting information about their activities and analysing its significance. Both managers are now attending a meeting to argue the case for creating the new post. They expect to meet some opposition from colleagues who fear the company could move into the dangerous waters of industrial espionage.

COST-BENEFIT ANALYSIS: DOES COMPUTING PAY?

Westmeath has a small but flexible computer system which handles the payroll and personnel records. The Production Manager now wants to extend the system to cover stock control. This will cost money, so he must show that it will be cost-effective—that is, that it will make (or save) more than it costs. He has therefore drawn up the following analysis to show what he believes his project will achieve.

PROJECT	Stock control
DATE	26 Jan 1990
DESCRIPTION	To maintain stock control records, requisitioning and other issues

SUMMARY

Project **live** (months)	9
Break-even point (months)	21
Cumulative benefit 24 mths (£K)	3.7
Cumulative benefit 36 mths (£K)	60.9
Maximum net investment (£K)	40.4

	1st year				2nd year				3rd year			
	1	2	3	4	1	2	3	4	1	2	3	4
1 Development costs												
1.1 Systems and programming	3.0	13.4	5.3	–	–	–	–	–	–	–	–	–
1.2 Machine time	–	0.6	0.7	–	–	–	–	–	–	–	–	–
1.3 Other	–	0.4	0.6	–	–	–	–	–	–	–	–	–
2 Running costs												
2.1 Data preparation	–	–	–	1.2	1.4	1.4	1.6	1.6	1.6	2.0	2.0	2.0
2.2 Machine time	–	–	–	9.6	10.0	10.0	11.0	11.0	11.0	12.0	12.0	12.0
2.3 Clerical effort	–	–	3.0	2.5	2.5	2.5	2.5	2.5	2.5	2.5	3.0	3.0
2.4 Program maintenance	–	–	–	0.6	0.6	0.6	0.6	0.6	0.6	0.6	1.0	1.0
3 Total expenditure (£K)	3.0	14.4	9.6	13.9	14.5	14.5	15.7	15.7	15.7	17.1	18.0	18.0
4 Cumulative expenditure (£K)	3.0	17.4	27.0	40.9	55.4	69.9	85.6	101.3	117.0	134.1	152.1	170.1
5 Total benefits (£K)	–	–	–	3.0	12.0	30.0	30.0	30.0	30.0	32.0	32.0	32.0
6 Cumulative benefits (£K)	–	–	–	3.0	15.0	45.0	75.0	105.0	135.0	167.0	199.0	231.0
7 Cash flow (£K)	(3.0)	(14.4)	(9.6)	(10.9)	(2.5)	15.5	14.3	14.3	14.3	14.9	14.0	14.0
8 Cumulative cash flow (£K)	(3.0)	(17.4)	(27.0)	(37.9)	(40.4)	(24.9)	(10.6)	3.7	18.0	32.9	46.9	60.9

Consider the Production Manager's figures and answer these questions:

1. If work on the project begins on 1 August 1990, and if it goes according to schedule, when will the project
   (a) start producing useful information for Stock Control?
   (b) reach its maximum net investment figure?
   (c) start to make more money per quarter than it costs?
   (d) start to show a return on total investment?

2. How have the figures in the Summary (top right-hand corner) been arrived at?

3. If you had to authorize this project, what further information might you demand before you signed the proposal?

4. How would you show these figures on a graph?

THE RIGHT WORDS IN THE RIGHT PLACE

Alarmed by what is happening at the Westmeath factory, two senior executives from Karlstad-Poly have announced their intention of flying to Ireland immediately for an on-the-spot investigation. McLaren is furious, but realizes that his visitors will need to be handled with tact and diplomacy. He discusses with his Production Manager what line he should take.

> In the example, you can see how McLaren rephrases his remarks when he talks to his visitors from Sweden. Rewrite the other remarks in the same way.

Example

Production Manager: What are you going to say to these people from Karlstad?

McLaren Oh well—I'll have to express appreciation, I suppose; after all, they're taking the trouble to come here, which in a way is pretty nice of them, considering.

Well, gentlemen—I'd like to start by thanking you both for coming here—it's very good of you . . .

1 Then I guess I'll outline the problem as we see it—anxiety about jobs, people getting hold of the wrong end of the stick or getting upset because they can't make out what's going on . . .

2 They're not stupid, these Swedes. They must have had to face up to this kind of situation at home, and if they can cope, I don't see why we shouldn't.

3 For the time being, though, I'm going to tell these people they've just got to play ball with us. They've got to let our lot know what's happening and what they're planning, so we can get rid of all this distrust and clear the air a bit.

4 After all, our workers are reasonable enough, as long as you treat them right. They know things have got to change, but of course, like all of us, they're apt to turn against you if you rub them up the wrong way . . . That's what I'm going to say!

WRITTEN ASSIGNMENT

The strike at Westmeath Kitchen Equipment is unofficial, and the strikers want to get back to work as soon as possible. First, however, they want to get their union to recognize their grievance and open negotiations with the Westmeath management, seeking certain guarantees concerning redundancy and automation. The union is the Amalgamated Shop-Floor Workers' Association (ASFWA). The link between the Union and its members at Westmeath is the Works Convener. He is a full-time employee of the company, and also the elected representative of all its Union members. His principal duty is to call members together—that is, to convene meetings; hence his title. The Works Convener has explained the whole problem to ASFWA Regional Office on the telephone, but he has been asked to put it on paper as well, for the record.

> Draft the Works Convener's report for him, basing its contents mainly on the poster which is reproduced in the Casebook and which has now been put on display on the company's notice-boards. (For notes on report writing, see Appendix, section 4.)

A PARTISAN REPORT

This report aims to enlist union sympathy; there is nothing impartial or unbiased about it. But it will do this more effectively if it is expressed in moderate, factual terms. It will be sent to the Union's Regional Office.

PRESENTATION

Give the report a title. Explain why it is being written and exactly what information it will give. Then say where the information came from. In this case, it will have been obtained from articles in the local press, and from statements made by your own management, who do their best to keep everyone up-to-date. You may also decide to mention that some of the information is based on guesswork.

MAKING FIGURES TELL

In your *Findings*, refer briefly to the takeover by Karlstad-Poly and the government plan to give investment grants, but do not describe these in detail. Then present the estimates that are shown on the poster. You could do this in the following way:

(i) Write a paragraph on *The effects of automation* and say, in sub-paragraphs, what changes will take place in the product range, in fabrication, in assembly, in packing. Mention the processes that will be affected.

(ii) Write a further paragraph about how the labour force will be affected. Devise a table to show the numbers of workers, of different grades, in each department before and after automation is introduced. Then—your most telling point of all—make it clear that well over 300 jobs are likely to be lost: four-fifths of the workforce!

ENDING THE REPORT

Conclude by making recommendations. You want ASFWA to seek guarantees from the management (decide exactly what these should be). As soon as these negotiations begin, everyone will go back to work; no one wants the strike to last a day longer than it has to.

Alternative assignment

Here is a simple diagram of the *Westmix Junior* hand-held mixer. It should be more or less self-explanatory (the release button, when pressed, pushes the whisks out of their holders so that they can be washed). However, brief instructions are enclosed with each new mixer. These first congratulate the buyer on choosing a Westmeath product, then tell him or her how to put the whisks into the holder, how to use the mixer, how to look after it, and how to clean it. A few important *DO*s and *DON'T*s are also included. Write the instruction sheet, referring the reader to the diagram when necessary.

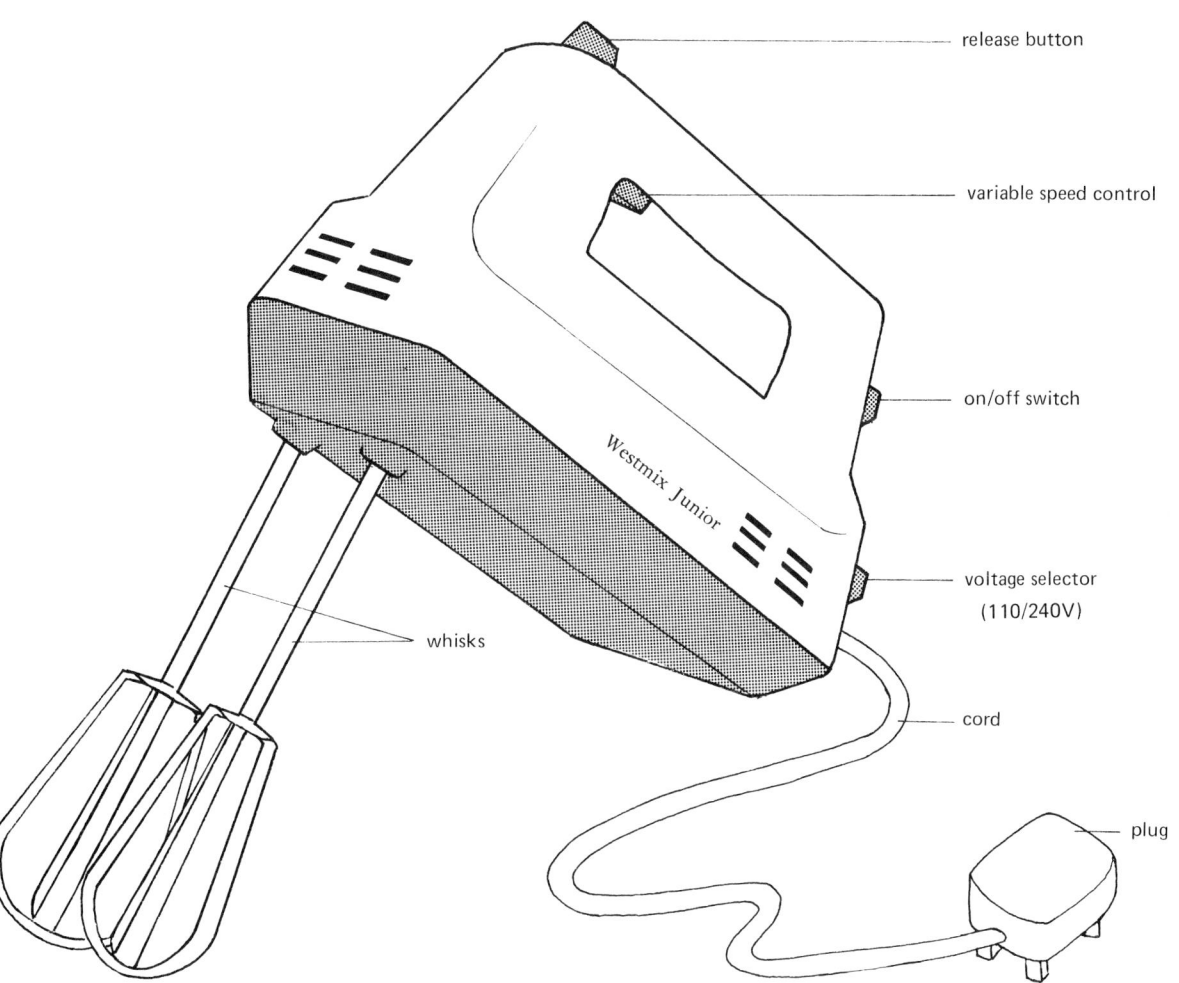

HEARD IN THE WORKS CANTEEN

Karlstad have a scheme to give shares in the company as productivity bonuses.
Well, why not? It gives people a stake in the firm.

The foreman sent the new apprentice to Stores today, to ask for some glass nails and a rubber hammer.
That's an old one. But it always works, if you get a lad who's slow on the uptake.

How's Patrick getting on at his new school?
Well, he's just about holding his own in class—but then studying never was his strong point.

How did they get rid of that useless Production Manager?
Early retirement; you know—a golden handshake.

So everyone in this firm eats together: blue-collar and white-collar workers?
That's right. It's supposed to promote togetherness among the staff.

Next time you're in Stockholm, give me a ring. We can have lunch together.
Thanks! I'll take you up on that.

What do you think of this plan to instal a word processor? It'll do the work of six typists!
It's the thin end of the wedge. We'll all be laid off in six months.

There hasn't been much growth in the last six years, I notice.
Well, we were hard hit by the world trade recession. We pulled through that, but then we started having cash-flow problems.

Have you heard the latest? Joe had an accident on his way home last night.
Is he all right?
He's fine, but the car's a complete write-off.

Ever thought of changing your job?
Funny you should say that. I've been putting out a few feelers lately . . .

1 Find out what these idioms mean.
2 How would you express these ideas without using an idiom?
3 Write your own dialogues including these idioms correctly and appropriately used.

TANSKIN

UNDERSTANDING THE CASE

Read the case study in the Casebook and answer these questions.

1. What attracts Swiss buyers to Tanskin products?
2. Why is Sanderson so complacent about his firm's performance in Switzerland?
3. How does Duthli shatter this complacency?
4. Why does Sanderson talk to Blunt about 'a tremendous opportunity' and 'a real breakthrough'?
5. What is Blunt's immediate reaction to Sanderson's remarks about 'someone with a better design background'? Why does he react in this way?
6. Why is Round not unduly worried about his firm's low profits in Switzerland?
7. What is the attitude of the other senior executives toward the Export Manager, Arthur Round?
8. Why does Round react as he does to the suggestion that Tanskin should appoint an agent in Switzerland?
9. Why does Round write to Sanderson from Stockholm? What does he hope to gain if his suggestion is accepted?
10. Where does Tanskin's real problem lie—in Switzerland, or in its own Head Office in Manchester?

VOCABULARY Shooting down Arthur Round's proposal

John Holroyd, the Company Secretary, is lunching with Alfred Blunt in the Managers' Dining Room. Fill in the gaps in their remarks from the box, in the usual way.

Holroyd I'm afraid Arthur is a bit of an empire-builder.

Blunt Mm. His idea of an Export D_____ is quite a good one, if we can make it c_____-e_____. It could have a dramatic _____ on the p_____ of our overseas operations.

Holroyd Maybe. But it would involve a big _____; it would be a serious d_____ on our r_____, at least during the first year or two of o_____. It would need a _____ of at least three people, and probably we'd have to set up a permanent sales _____ overseas.

To get the thing off the ground this year, we'd have to a_____ money that's already been earmarked for other departmental b_____s. I really don't think they can s_____ it.

Blunt But the new department would start to _____ to our r_____ more or less immediately. I don't see why it shouldn't b_____ _____ in two or three years.

Holroyd It would make us short of c_____, and cash-_____ problems are what every accountant dreads. We must maintain sufficient l_____ in the firm to keep us out of trouble if our _____ suddenly ask us to settle all our d_____. No, no, it's just not on. The e_____ would be out of all proportion to the b_____. We can't _____ to make mistakes on such a scale . . .

benefit	creditor	effect
budget	department	effective
cash	force	flow
cost	operation	impact
debt	staff	
drain		
	afford	
expenditure	allocate	
liquidity	break even	
outlay	contribute	
profitability	spare	
resource		
revenue		

THINGS ARE NOT ALWAYS WHAT THEY SEEM

Herr Duthli is chatting to the representative of a Yugoslav leather goods manufacturer, Eva Celnič. He has just seen something in an English newspaper that amuses him.

Duthli Here, what do you make of this ad in the London Observer? 'A leading manufacturer of leather goods is seeking an Overseas Sales Representative...' I bet you that's Tanskin!

Celnič What makes you think that? It could be anyone.

Duthli Oh, something that their Mr Sanderson said to me just now. Considering what a mess their firm is in, I shouldn't have thought they were in a position to expand their staff.

Celnič Well!—if they're advertising for overseas reps, they can hardly be on the edge of bankruptcy.

Duthli Judging from what I've seen of them, Tanskin are going to have their work cut out to stay in business.

Celnič That's not how I see it at all. Their interim results for the first half of the year are excellent.

Duthli Oh? How do you know? You don't even work for them!

Celnič Exactly. That's all the more reason why I should keep track of what they're doing. According to the report published in the Financial News, Tanskin look like having record pre-tax profits this year.

Duthli Oh—do they! In that case, why are they cutting their prices?

Celnič Cutting their prices?

Duthli Right across the board. Now what conclusion do you draw from that?—I'll tell you how I see it! All the signs are that Tanskin is being forced back on to the defensive in its marketing strategy! How else would you explain it?

Celnič You may be right, up to a point. But I'd say that price-cutting on that scale is just as likely to be a sign of confidence... Can I see that advertisement?

Duthli Of course—here it is.

Celnič H'mm. Apparently, I'm just the sort of person they're after... I think I ought to apply for this. Thank you very much, Herr Duthli—good night!

Duthli Huh... It just goes to show that one shouldn't jump to conclusions...

1 Listen again and find as many expressions as possible which are used to draw conclusions, or jump to them, sometimes without good reason.
2 Practise the expressions recorded after the dialogue on the tape.
3 With the following check-list to help you, do the role-playing exercise.

DRAWING CONCLUSIONS—AND JUMPING TO THEM

I bet you that's...

Considering..., I shouldn't have thought...

They can hardly be...

Judging from what I've seen,...

According to..., they look like ——ing...

I'd say that that's a sign of...

Role-playing exercise

Three months ago, Quagga, the well-known toy manufacturers, launched a new product: a model locomotive driven by real steam. Quagga expected to sell 10,000 units in the Christmas period. Now, shortly after Christmas, it is clear that the model has flopped. About 7,500 unsold units remain in the firm's warehouse. The Manager is meeting his senior sales staff to explain what he thinks went wrong. After hearing his analysis, the staff will discuss what they can learn from the disaster.

AN INCENTIVE FOR THE SALES FORCE

Tanskin depends for its excellent UK sales figures on its staff of highly motivated salesmen and women. Apart from a generous commission, these people enjoy several other fringe benefits. One of these is the *Salesman of the Year* award scheme. At the end of each year, the Head of UK Sales, Julian Courtauld, picks the three outstanding members of his staff. The winner gets a holiday for two in the sun, and the runners-up receive substantial cash prizes.

Choosing the winners is never easy. Courtauld takes into account all the information in the table which you see below. Who would you recommend for first, second and third prizes this year?

NAME etc.	Sales target (£000)	Value of sales (£000)	Performance compared with previous year (%)	New accounts obtained	Days absent from work	REMARKS
WEINBERG ** [17] A	150	160	+8	6	12	Previous winner.
BERRIMAN ** [11] A	200	180	-8	10	6	Once again, excellent sales in last quarter of year.
CARPENTER (Mrs) * [1] D	35	40	-	-	6	New area: provisionally classified as D.
ACKROYD ** [8] B	125	110	-15	0	10	Previous winner and second place.
MASKIE (Mrs) * [3] D	55	65	+6	4	22	Marriage broken up - custody problem.
DALTON * [8] A	170	200	+15	8	2	Twice a previous winner.
GEBLER **** [25] C	80	88	+18	0	5	Retires in two years.
HAMPSON **** [14] B	80	95	+12	6	10	Best dressed and most punctual.
PETRIE ** [2] D	60	60	+3	3	18	Went on one-week sales course in February.
CAPES (Mrs) *** [9] A	155	140	-15	2	18	Son killed in car crash.
HALL **** [16] C	100	77	-14	0	15	Asked to be transferred to another area.

Key   Age: over 50   ****   Grading of sales area: A = excellent potential
                 40 - 49   ***   B = good   "
                 30 - 39   **   C = average   "
                 under 30   *   D = limited   "

Years of service with Tanskin: [17]

THE RIGHT WORDS IN THE RIGHT PLACE

John Holroyd, Company Secretary of Tanskin, has a Personal Assistant who has been with the firm for years and who knows as much about it as any of the senior managers. He frequently relies on her memory and her tact when his own fail. This conversation supplies a good example of such reliance. It is 4 pm on a Friday, and Holroyd is about to depart to catch the Intercity train to London.

> Below, you can see the beginning of Mary's telephone message to Mr Smithson, and the instructions on which it is based. Write the rest of what she said on the phone, giving Mr Smithson all the necessary information and leaving him with the feeling that the lunch was really a great success and well worth while.

Mary Oh, I meant to ask you, Mr Holroyd—did you enjoy your lunch with Mr Smithson?

Holroyd Oh my goodness—what a good thing you reminded me—I promised the old fool I'd write to him before the weekend. Look, could you ring him for me as soon as I've gone? Thank him for the lunch—nice to see him again, all the usual nonsense—hope his daughter passed her exam—he talked about nothing else all through the main course; it was incredibly boring and the food was awful, but of course his firm are very mean with expenses. In the end he came to the point. You've got his telephone number, have you?

Mary Hulme 334782.

Holroyd Yes. Well, he's got some crackpot notion for setting up a group pension scheme—you know he's a partner in a firm of insurance brokers—it's a scheme for firms that employ a large number of craftsmen and highly skilled workers. He thought he might be able to soft-soap me into recommending that we should join. So if you could just express my regrets—hope we meet again soon—is that my taxi outside?

Mary But Mr Holroyd! What reasons shall I give him for turning down his idea?

Holroyd Er—oh—number of craftsmen diminishing as we become more mechanized and less labour-intensive; no redundancies, of course, just natural wastage. Majority of the workforce already well advanced in years—wouldn't be an economic proposition to—er—extend their pension rights. Think of the premiums we'd have to pay! You could mention our part-time workers as well; they aren't eligible for company pensions at all.

Mary But he'll just tell me they ought to be!

Holroyd Out of the question. You tell me one other company that pays superannuation to part-timers!

Mary But there was that man who lost his finger; he got a disability pension.

Holroyd Oh yes, that's another matter altogether. So far as industrial accidents are concerned, we're fully covered by old Smithson's firm already. Poor old boy, he's past it really. For heaven's sake make it very clear to him that we are not interested. I explained it all to him over coffee in the hotel dining room, but of course he was too sleepy to listen by that time. Have a nice weekend—see you on Tuesday. Goodbye!

Mary Good afternoon. May I speak to Mr Smithson, please? . . . Hello, Mr Smithson. This is Mary Senior, Mr Holroyd's Personal Assistant at Tanskin. Mr Holroyd asked me to ring you to tell you how much he enjoyed your lunch together last week. He's been called away suddenly, otherwise he would have telephoned you himself.

WRITTEN ASSIGNMENT

At tea-time on Friday afternoon, Derek Sanderson clears out his In-tray and finds the following:

(i) a letter from the local representative of the British International Advisory Council, asking permission for a group of executives from leather-working cooperatives in Yugoslavia to tour the factory on 17 November;

(ii) an anonymous note, taken from the Suggestions Box in the canteen, complaining that a lot of private car owners drive dangerously on their way from the main road to the works car park behind the factory;

(iii) a note written by Sanderson himself, as a reminder that Arthur Round's report on his trip to Austria is required urgently—in time for circulation to the Board before their next meeting;

(iv) a plaintive letter from an employee, Mavis Scott, who applied to the Personnel Manager for time off with pay (one day a week for a year) to attend a marketing course at the local College of Further Education; her request has been turned down without any satisfactory reason being given.

Imagine you are Derek Sanderson. You are keen to get home early, but determined to deal with all these matters before you leave the office. Write short memos to:

(i) Alfred Blunt, Production Manager (Yugoslav visitors)
(ii) Charles White, Safety Officer (dangerous drivers)
(iii) Arthur Round, Export Manager (overdue report)
(iv) Lesley Winton, Personnel Manager (Miss Scott's marketing course).

Then write a brief letter to Miss Scott, taking care not to commit yourself to anything at this stage.

Alternative assignment

Tanskin are finally bringing on to the market a new, ultra-fashionable brief-case designed for the ambitious junior executive. The name chosen for the product is *Meteor*. This is meant to convey the impression that any executive possessing this particular case will inevitably shoot to the top in his chosen career! As part of the publicity material for this item, Tanskin are producing a special sales leaflet. The publicity photographs have already been taken. All that remains is to write the accompanying text—or 'copy', to use the technical term. It is your task to carry out this part of the publicity assignment.

HEARD NEAR THE RECEPTION DESK

Tell me the whole story.
Well, it's long and complicated. To put it in a nutshell: I gather that he left his last job under a bit of a cloud...

I told him I still didn't agree.
That's right. Stick to your guns. He'll come round to our way of thinking in the end.

Twenty per cent market share isn't bad.
It's not good enough. We could corner the market in that area if we tried.

I'm a bit concerned about our sales effort in Belgium. We're not using the right approach. In a sophisticated luxury market, the hard sell just doesn't work.
Well, we tried the soft sell and that flopped too.

How would you like to organize the annual staff outing to Weston-super-Mare?
No thanks, I've got enough on my plate.

Very stylish reception area you've got here, James.
Yes, well—just window-dressing, you know. It's supposed to impress the customers.

Hello! I thought you were away this week.
Yes, I was going to Caracas, but it fell through.

Have you finished drafting the copy for that new sales brochure?
I've been racking my brains all morning—I just can't make it sound right.

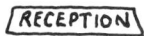

I hear the Factory Manager's getting people's backs up a bit.
Well, in the three weeks that he's been here, he's certainly been throwing his weight around.

What on earth are all these ski-caps doing here? Weren't we going to get someone to take them off our hands as a job lot?
Yes, but they seem to be rather slow in coming to pick them up.

1 Find out what these idioms mean.
2 How would you express these ideas without using an idiom?
3 Write your own dialogues including these idioms correctly and appropriately used.

BLIK

UNDERSTANDING THE CASE
Read the case study in the Casebook and answer these questions.

1. Who owns the shares of Blik (Bakumba) at the moment?
2. What is the difference between indigenization and nationalization?
3. What is the ultimate purpose of the Bakumba Government's indigenization policy?
4. What other Government decree is likely to affect Blik? How might it affect Blik's decision with regard to indigenization?
5. What special reason does Blik have for fearing indigenization?
6. What is Blik's purpose in continuing to trade in Bakumba?
7. Why is Blik (Bakumba) anxious about its share values?
8. Why did Feinburg ask Mrozek for advice?
9. Does Mrozek seem to think that, on the whole, Blik should give way to Government pressure or attempt to negotiate?
10. If Blik decides to fight the decree, what arguments or weapons does it have to hand?

VOCABULARY Looking at the balance sheet

Julius Feinburg Jr is being interviewed on Bakumba TV in a programme called *This Is Your Business*. He has been asked to explain what the term 'shareholders' funds' means in the company's results as they were published today in the *Bakumba Mail*. Fill in the gaps in his remarks in the usual way.

Feinburg 'Shareholders' funds': well, that means all the money that the shareholders have i_____ in the b_____, whether it's in o_____ shares or in p_____ that have been r_____ in the firm. Such profits are usually called r_____.

The reason that shareholders' funds are down this year is that we paid an exceptionally high d_____ to our o_____ s_____. As you can see, p_____ were right down, from 22 million to under 8 million. It's true that we paid rather less i_____ this year on our b_____, but that was because interest r_____ fell.

We actually increased the total _____ of our funded debt; that means long-_____ debts which are regarded as permanent f_____ and listed among the l_____ of the company.

Admittedly the last twelve months has been an unusual _____, and some of these f_____ are a bit artificial. We've recently _____ a s_____ s_____ of money in new plant, and so far we've had no _____ on our c_____.

borrowing	business	period
capital	invest	term
dividend	shareholder	time
interest		
liability	amount	ordinary
profit	figure	retained
rate	funds	substantial
reserve	sum	
return		

TALKING ABOUT THE FUTURE

Read or listen to the dialogue.

Ella Swale and Yves Bertaud have come to the Ministry of Economic Development for talks with one of the Minister's aides, Colonel Sumbawan.

Sumbawan I'd like to start by asking you—how do you see Blik's operations in Bakumba developing, over, say, the next ten years?

Swale Taking indigenization into account, or not?

Sumbawan Let's leave it out for the moment. I'm afraid it will only complicate the issue.

Swale Yes, I agree. Well, briefly, our projections of demand and raw material prices lead us to believe that the market is approaching saturation point.

Sumbawan Really? You predict that the demand for soft drinks will drop off?

Bertaud Oh no; just that, in the foreseeable future, it'll stop growing. Look at this chart. You can see that the demand curve is flattening out. But the prices curve rises steeply, and it'll go on rising.

Sumbawan So—it looks as if Blik will price themselves out of the market!

Bertaud Not necessarily, because wages and the standard of living are likely at least to keep pace with prices. Real wages should rise as the economy develops.

Swale Be that as it may, you can see from these figures how we plan to expand production by diversifying into other fields. By 1994, total investment will have topped the three-million mark. Production will be running at a million cans a week, thirty per cent of which will be for export.

Sumbawan H'mm. According to your published results for 1989 in the *Bakumba Mail*, the investment is declining in value.

Bertaud An untypical year, Colonel. We're confident that the economic climate will improve rapidly. Our new bottling plant should break even within two years.

Swale All the same, we reckon there are plenty of problems ahead. We're forecasting a production shortfall this year of half a million cans. Next year, there seems certain to be an acute shortage of tinplate...

Sumbawan You appreciate that the disappointing results last year may well have an adverse effect on share prices...

Swale Ah! But indigenization will send share values rocketing up, Colonel—just you wait and see!

1. Listen again and find as many expressions as possible which are used for talking about the future, particularly when forecasts are based on statistical evidence or the extrapolation of present trends.
2. Practise the expressions recorded after the dialogue on the tape.
3. With the following check-list to help you, do the role-playing exercise.

FORECASTING

...lead us to believe that...

It looks as if...will...

Not necessarily!...are likely to...

They may well have an effect on...

By..., it will have ——ed...

It will be ——ing...

It should...within...

Role-playing exercise

Two senior Blik executives have agreed to meet reporters from the *Bakumba Mail* for an in-depth interview. The reporters are particularly interested in the probable effects of indigenization on the company's future, above all on its plans for new investment and diversification. They have well-formed ideas of their own, which the Blik managers may confirm, correct or contradict.

THE BALANCE SHEET—A DISCOURAGING PICTURE?

Under Bakumban law, Blik has to publish its results at the end of every fiscal year. Early in October, this advertisement appeared in the *Bakumba Mail*.

BLIK (BAKUMBA) PTE.

Results for Year Ended 30 September 1989

(in Bakumban currency, taking 100 emirs = US$3.75 approx.)

Year ended 30.9.88 (E 000s)		Year ended 30.9.89 (E 000s)
22,626	Gross profit (turnover 265,953)	7,915
7,031	Licensing agreements	5,196
3,200	Investments	239
32,857		13,350
3,834	Less interest on debt	3,476
29,023	Profit before taxation	9,874
21,673	Profit after taxation etc.	5,112
E48.20	Earnings per Ordinary Share	E37.60
E11.84	Ordinary Dividend	E 9.24

Abbreviated Balance Sheet

247,815	Fixed Assets	218,693
11,318	Cost of patents and licences	11,007
3,997	Investment	2,654
214,735	Current Assets	189,724
477,865		422,078
210,678	Current Liabilities	191,505
27,126	Long-term provisions and creditors	25,145
101,230	Funded debt	120,628
138,831	SHAREHOLDERS' FUNDS AND DEFERRED TAXATION	84,800
77,865		422,078

NOTE: The above figures are subject to final audit.

Study these figures, compare the results for last year and this year, and say why you think the figures will make the value of Blik (Bakumba) shares fall.

THE RIGHT WORDS IN THE RIGHT PLACE

Robert Shafto is an American who until recently was Finance Director of Blik (Bakumba). He is now in London, where David Sylvester, a journalist, finds him and asks him for an interview. Shafto agrees, on condition his name is not mentioned in Sylvester's article. The interview covers many topics; here is a transcript of one part of it.

Sylvester . . . Now tell me, Bob—what makes you so sure Blik are going to be able to dodge this new ruling about forty per cent Bakumban ownership?

Shafto Er . . . Three things. First, Blik provide a lot of jobs. If Julius Feinburg decided to throw in his hand and pull the outfit out of the country, that would have quite a sizeable impact on the local economy.

True—Blik are able to employ a lot of people because wages are low. But they do give their workers a decent living wage, and they have subsidized housing, things like that.

Of course, if Blik went, the Bakumban Government could say OK, we'll step in and take over the bottling plants and whatnot, and they could start up a completely new corporation—but I don't think they'll be in a hurry to do that. They've got enough on their plate as it is.

Second reason: Blik are underpinning the economy in more ways than one. The firm pays taxes—brings in massive quantities of foreign currency. Never mind what Central Government says, the local authorities aren't going to be keen to wave goodbye to several million US dollars a year.

Thirdly—er . . . well, thirdly, I think they're bluffing. It's just a hunch, but I reckon that if it really comes to the point, then the Government will back down.

Sylvester So you don't think Blik should pull out of Bakumba?

Shafto Ah!—I didn't say that! . . .

Here is part of Sylvester's article, based very closely on what Shafto ('*a former senior executive of a large American-owned corporation*') told him. Continue the article for him, on the same lines.

My informant also explained why he believed that Blik had little to fear from the Bakumban Government's recent decree that foreign businesses must transfer 40 per cent of their shares to Bakumban nationals. He pointed out, first, that . . .

WRITTEN ASSIGNMENT

As soon as a decision has been made about Blik's strategy in Bakumba, Julius Feinburg despatches a telex to the offices of Blik Corporation (USA), the parent company. Draft the text of this for him, basing it on the decision which you have made.

MAKING THEM SEE

This telex is not a matter of a dozen words. Feinburg, like many heads of foreign missions, has very little faith in Head Office's understanding of the local situation. Whatever has been decided, he must obtain their ungrudging cooperation and support. Therefore, he must explain the decision in detail.

The message will be marked:
ATTENTION VICE-PRESIDENT FOOD PRODUCTS DIVISION

Say immediately what topic the message is concerned with:
RE BAKUMBA GOVERNMENT DECREE . . .

Then say who took the decision and what they decided:
MANAGEMENT OF BLIK (BAKUMBA) TODAY DECIDED . . .

Then say what they decided to do—and why:
. . . FOR THESE REASONS:
1. . . .

Of course, you can tabulate points in a telex message just as you can in a typewritten document.

Finally, say what you expect to happen next and what help you want. Perhaps there will be no further developments for several months—or perhaps you will be summoned tomorrow to the Ministry of Economic Development for urgent talks with Colonel Sumbawan! If you think you are going to need assistance of any kind, as you almost certainly will—information, money, authority to sell shares or put the company into liquidation, a good corporation lawyer or just some advice —then ask for it.

Alternative assignment

Ahmad Jaffar is a wealthy Bakumban businessman (one of the 'new middle class' mentioned in Hanna Mrozek's letter) who is thinking seriously of buying shares in Blik (Bakumba), if, indeed, Blik eventually decide to give way to the Government decree. He would probably buy ten or twenty thousand dollars' worth—not enough to make him a major shareholder, but still an investment to be made with caution. He wants a second opinion on the soundness of the company, and writes to an old friend, Virgil Blunt, who lives in Bakumba and whose judgement Jaffar trusts. Write the letter that Blunt sends to Jaffar in reply, advising him about his proposed purchase of shares. Your opinion will be based mainly on the published results for the past two years. (See above.)

HEARD IN THE ANTE-ROOM

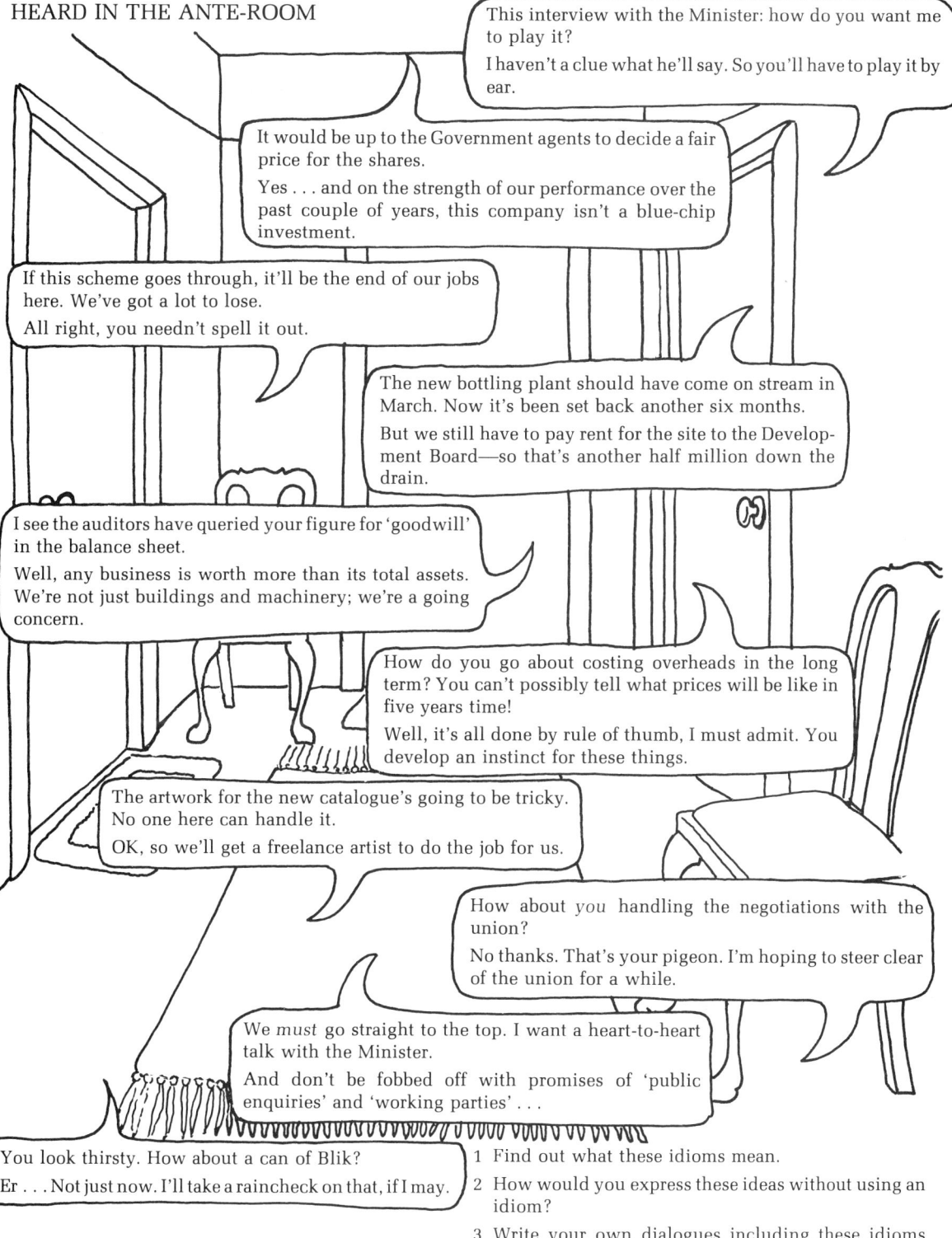

This interview with the Minister: how do you want me to play it?
I haven't a clue what he'll say. So you'll have to play it by ear.

It would be up to the Government agents to decide a fair price for the shares.
Yes . . . and on the strength of our performance over the past couple of years, this company isn't a blue-chip investment.

If this scheme goes through, it'll be the end of our jobs here. We've got a lot to lose.
All right, you needn't spell it out.

The new bottling plant should have come on stream in March. Now it's been set back another six months.
But we still have to pay rent for the site to the Development Board—so that's another half million down the drain.

I see the auditors have queried your figure for 'goodwill' in the balance sheet.
Well, any business is worth more than its total assets. We're not just buildings and machinery; we're a going concern.

How do you go about costing overheads in the long term? You can't possibly tell what prices will be like in five years time!
Well, it's all done by rule of thumb, I must admit. You develop an instinct for these things.

The artwork for the new catalogue's going to be tricky. No one here can handle it.
OK, so we'll get a freelance artist to do the job for us.

How about *you* handling the negotiations with the union?
No thanks. That's your pigeon. I'm hoping to steer clear of the union for a while.

We *must* go straight to the top. I want a heart-to-heart talk with the Minister.
And don't be fobbed off with promises of 'public enquiries' and 'working parties' . . .

You look thirsty. How about a can of Blik?
Er . . . Not just now. I'll take a raincheck on that, if I may.

1 Find out what these idioms mean.
2 How would you express these ideas without using an idiom?
3 Write your own dialogues including these idioms correctly and appropriately used.

KRETEK

UNDERSTANDING THE CASE

Read the case study in the Casebook and answer these questions.

1. How successful has Steven van Dam been in his business career to date?
2. What kind of relationship does Steven have with Sanusi?
3. How does Steven's attitude to business probably differ from Sanusi's?
4. Who is Mrs Subroto? Why is she interested in Steven's proposition?
5. Why is Steven initially very confident about the market potential of *kretek* cigarettes in the UK?
6. What lesson did Steven learn from his difficulties with the customs officer?
7. Why might the Department of Trade and Industry (DTI) regard cloves in cigarettes as an 'unacceptable additive'?
8. Mr Day, the solicitor, suggests that Steven may have to produce evidence to show that the cloves mixed with the tobacco are not harmful. What sort of evidence could Steven produce, and how would he obtain it?
9. Give brief details of the legal and financial problems in this case.
10. What conclusions have you drawn about the character of Steven van Dam?

VOCABULARY Situations, procedures and proceedings

Steven van Dam is on the telephone to his travel agent, making arrangements for his next trip. Fill in the gaps in his remarks from the box below.

Van Dam I want a hotel r_____ for three nights in Singapore, and a _____ for a flight to Bangkok on the twentieth. How much is the air _____, by the way? . . .

Right. Now the next leg of the _____ is to Kabul. . . . Yes, I know I need a _____ to enter the country. Can you tell me, what's the p_____ for getting one? . . .

The next thing I wanted to ask you about is air c_____. I want to a_____-f_____ some perishable goods to the UK from Indonesia, and I want to know the r_____ per kilo . . . How many kilos? Oh, I see; I thought you just _____ so much per kilo . . . Well, I'm not really in a _____ to say exactly. It depends on the c_____. I'll probably have a t_____ r_____ first, say thirty kilos . . .

Later, he talks to a friend about the problems and rewards of leading the kind of life he does.

Van Dam Why do I do it? Well, it's all ex____. I just enjoy t_____. I'm going to import a small quantity of these *kretek* cigarettes first, as a kind of p_____ p_____, just to _____ the market. If I can get an import _____ for that, I should be able to get one for a bigger consignment. We'll just have to try it out and see what happens. If necessary, I'll bring a t_____ _____ against the Customs and Excise, but I don't think that s_____ will ever arise. They'd have to _____ that the cigarettes contained a harmful drug. I certainly don't want to start legal _____. I'd only have to pay enormous f_____ to some lawyer.

booking	air cargo	circumstances
journey	allowance	position
reservation	experience	situation
travel	licence	
travelling	permission	pilot project
	permit	test case
charge		trial run
cost	procedure	
fare	proceedings	air-freight
fee	process	demonstrate
rate		prove

FIRST MEETING WITH MRS SUBROTO

Read or listen to the dialogue.

Steven van Dam is talking to Mrs Subroto in her house in Java.

Subroto So, Mr van Dam, you're interested in importing *kretek* cigarettes into England.

Van Dam Yes, that's the general idea. In fact, that was my reason for coming to Malang today.

Subroto What sort of quantities do you have in mind? The reason I ask is that our production capacity here is limited. My husband had very ambitious plans for the factory, but since he died, I have concentrated on maintaining the quality of the cigarettes. Any plans for expansion really depend on establishing a good export market.

Van Dam It seems to me you've achieved a great deal already . . . Anyway, my target to begin with would be to sell twenty thousand cigarettes a month.

Subroto Twenty thousand a month! It hardly seems worth the effort, does it? I shall have to charge a very high price to cover all my overheads, and then what sort of profit are you aiming at?

Van Dam Well—say a hundred and fifty to two hundred pounds—no, you're quite right, it doesn't make much sense. Suppose we say . . . two hundred thousand a month?

Subroto Well, that's going to the other extreme! I can't manage two hundred thousand a month, not yet. But from next January onwards I could let you have one hundred thousand.

Van Dam All right, if we can agree on the price. I can handle one hundred thousand, I'm certain. If everything works out as I've planned, I think we should set ourselves a goal of half a million a month. Then we'd both be getting somewhere!

Subroto Well, let's not overdo it. In order to meet your requirements I shall have to turn down new customers here, and will probably need to expand the factory. That's all right if you really do mean to go on buying from me, but if you lose interest after six months or so then *I* am the one who will have to start looking for alternative outlets.

Van Dam I see your point, Mrs Subroto, but don't worry. I've every intention of setting up this business on a permanent basis. All I want is to see you shipping your *kretek* cigarettes to London. I know they'll find a ready market—in fact, I'm going to make sure that they do!

1 Listen again and find as many expressions as possible which are used to talk about what you intend or hope to do.
2 Practise the expressions recorded after the dialogue on the tape.
3 With the following check-list to help you, do the role-playing exercise.

TALKING ABOUT AIMS, TARGETS, AMBITIONS

So you're interested in . . . ?

My reason for ——ing is to . . .

We're concentrating on . . .

My initial target is . . .

What sort of . . . are you aiming at?

I've every intention of ——ing . . .

The idea is to . . .

I plan to . . .

Role-playing exercise

A cigarette company finds itself in financial difficulties and, in an attempt to remedy the situation, appoints a new Sales Manager. He is to liaise with the Promotions Manager, also newly appointed, to suggest ways in which the company can improve its image and develop its UK and overseas sales. Three months later, the two managers meet the Chairman and Managing Director to explain their plan of action.

PROFIT OR LOSS?

Steven van Dam now has more information about the costs of importing *kretek* cigarettes into Britain. He is confident that he can easily sell 20,000 a month (that is, 1,000 packets of 20); he thinks he might be able to sell as many as 100,000 without adding very much to his distribution costs.

His figures are shown below on the back of an envelope, just as he jotted them down. Several currencies are involved: sterling, American dollars, and Indonesian rupiah (Rp). Current rates of exchange are approximately £1 = US$2 = Rp 1,200.

Work in pairs or small groups. Assume that Steven still plans to sell the cigarettes at a retail price of 80p for 20.

1. How much excise duty is payable on each pack of 20?
2. How much, approximately, will a consignment of 20,000 cigarettes cost, cif London? A consignment of 100,000?
3. Will he make a profit if he sells 20,000 a month at 80p a pack? If he sells 100,000?
4. If he sells at 80p a pack retail, how many cigarettes must he import in a consignment in order to break even?

1. Subroto's price — ex works:
   - 1st 5,000 cigarettes: Rp. 17,500 per 1,000
   - next 10,000 cigarettes: Rp. 12,500 per 1,000
   - thereafter: Rp. 7,500 per 1,000

2. Insurance + freight:
   - 20,000 cigarettes: US$ 100
   - 100,000 cigarettes: US$ 140

3. Distribution to retailers:
   - 20,000 cigarettes: £40
   - 100,000 cigarettes: £60

4. Overheads (travel expenses etc.)
   Say £1,200 per year

5. Excise duty:
   £9 per 1,000 cigarettes
   + 30% of retail price

6. Retailer's mark-up:
   up to 13½%
   Say 12½% of retail price

+ profit ... ? 10p. per pack
retail price —
? 80p – 90p per pack

THE RIGHT WORDS IN THE RIGHT PLACE

Steven van Dam has a friend in Thailand who is an agent for the import of motorcar accessories from a British company. One day Steven receives a letter from Thailand, enclosing a photocopy of the agency agreement. His friend complains that he finds the legal English of the agreement hard to follow, and that he needs to understand it because he is in some kind of dispute with his principal—that is, with the company on whose behalf he acts. Steven writes in reply, pointing out that in these circumstances it is best to consult a good lawyer. However, he explains some of the sections of the agreement as well as he can, in simple everyday English.

Part of Steven's letter is shown here. Write your own simplified version of what the sections of the agreement say.

Example
   Upon receipt by the Agent of any order for the goods the Agent shall immediately transmit such order to the Principal who (if such order is accepted by the Principal) will execute the same by supplying the goods direct to the Customer.
   This means that as soon as anyone gives you an order you must pass it on to the Principal in Britain. Then, if he is willing to supply the goods, he does so.

1 Upon the execution of any such order the Principal shall forward to the Agent a duplicate copy of the invoice sent with the goods to the customer and in like manner shall from time to time inform the Agent when payment is made by the customer to the Principal.

2 The Principal shall allow the Agent a commission of 12.5 per cent (based on FOB United Kingdom values) in respect of all orders obtained direct by the Agent in the area which have been accepted and executed by the Principal. The said commission shall be payable every three months on the amounts actually received by the Principal from the customers.

3 Should any dispute arise as to the amount of commission payable by the Principal to the Agent the same shall be settled by the Auditors for the time being of the Principal whose certificate shall be final and binding on both the Principal and the Agent.

4 All questions of difference whatsoever which may at any time hereafter arise between the parties hereto or their respective representatives touching these presents or the subject matter thereof or arising out of or in relation thereto respectively and whether as to construction or otherwise shall be referred to arbitration in England in accordance with the provision of the Arbitration Act 1950 or any reenactment or statutory modification thereof for the time being in force.

(From *Specimen Agency Agreements for Exporters*)

WRITTEN ASSIGNMENT

While Steven van Dam worries about the future of *kretek* cigarettes, other business goes on as usual. One of his regular suppliers is Mr Liu Yung Sin, of Bandung, Indonesia. Mr Liu deals in *kain batik*, lengths of fine cotton cloth gorgeously decorated by hand. (A *kain*, or cloth, measures about 2m × 0.80m.) Steven sells these top-quality *kain* to the best stores in Amsterdam and London, and by advertising them through a mail-order house.

> Draft a letter from Steven to Liu, apologizing for not visiting him last month; asking for a quotation for 600 *kain batik*; giving instructions for selection, packing and shipping; and proposing a change in the method of payment, following recent fluctuations in the exchange rates of sterling, Dutch guilders and Indonesian rupiah.

TONE AND CONTENT
Steven has met Liu several times, and the letter should be personal and friendly, but it must still be businesslike. Avoid sudden changes in tone, for example, from very personal to very formal.

The apology should be easy to write. You didn't go to Bandung because you went to Malang instead—you can tell Liu about this or not, as you wish.

THE QUOTATION
Tabulate your requirements so that Liu can see at a glance what you want.

There are three qualities of *kain*—A, B and C. You want 200 of each. Different styles come from different towns: you want equal quantities from Ceribon and Solo. You want assorted patterns (every hand-made *kain* is unique, after all), but mostly in traditional designs; only about 20 per cent of them should be modern.

PACKING AND SHIPPING
You had a problem with the last consignment. They were inadequately packed in waterproof paper in fibreboard cartons; two cartons were lost, and several more were damaged so that sea water got in and stained the cloth. This time, you want the whole lot in a single wooden packing-case, marked DAMTEX ROTTERDAM. You will arrange customs clearance at Rotterdam and forwarding of goods to their destination. The price quoted will therefore be cif Rotterdam.

PAYMENT
In the past you have either paid cash (in Bandung) or by irrevocable letter of credit in Liu's favour with the Indonesian Trade Bank. You would now prefer to pay in guilders direct to Liu's bank account in Amsterdam; his bank will only release the shipping documents when they get your cheque.

Alternative assignment

Steven feels that it is only fair to warn Mrs Subroto that he may be forced to delay, reduce or even cancel his first order for *kretek* cigarettes, and ask her if she wants to suggest alternative arrangements. (For example, she might say that if the order for January is postponed, it must be postponed for at least six months.) He has written two letters to her, but he has had no reply. He eventually decides to send her a cable. Write this cable for him. Remember that Steven will be reluctant to send a long (and therefore expensive) cable, but that the cable must be unambiguous and must not sound too blunt or impatient.

CARBONIDE

UNDERSTANDING THE CASE

Read the case study in the Casebook and answer these questions.

1 Why did residents of Newsea throw soot at Laurensen?
2 How many separate sources of pollution or danger are mentioned in the case study?
3 What is Mrs Fulton's ambition? How can the problems of Carbonide help her to fulfil it?
4 What positive contributions has the International Carbonide Corporation made to the town of Newsea?
5 What is Laurensen's attitude to the Newsea community?
6 Why do International Carbonide often appoint foreigners as heads of subsidiary companies?
7 How does geography contribute to Carbonide's difficulties in Newsea?
8 Why does Laurensen write to a public relations consultant?
9 What sort of 'backlash' does Barnum predict, and why?
10 What statements do the people of Newsea want to hear and what authority will make these statements credible?

VOCABULARY Pollution and public relations

Maggie Fulton, leader of the Residents' Action Committee, and Steven Barnum, public relations expert, both have strong feelings about Carbonide. Here, they are expressing these feelings to a journalist who is interviewing them. Fill the gaps in their comments by taking words from the box below.

Mrs Fulton When I was a little girl, you could catch fish in the river here. But the w_____ from the chemical factory has c_____ the water and _____ all the fish. My dad grew beautiful lettuces, but nowadays some of the f_____ from the factory are so t_____ that we're frightened there may be a _____ of brain d_____ to our children.

The old steelworks were dirty, but it was plain n_____ dirt, not like this, ruining the c_____ and filling people with n_____ chemicals. The steel company never did anyone any _____; or if they did at least they paid fair _____.

Barnum Well, of course there's some lovely _____ in this part of the world, and we must convince people that caring for the e_____ is a top priority with Carbonide. They have an excellent record as c_____ in a number of countries, and they're very keen to promote their i_____ as a responsible and public-spirited company.

I'm sorry to say that there are certain p_____ _____ who seek to undermine public _____ in Carbonide's good _____. We've just issued a p_____ _____ about the work that Newsea Chemicals is doing to keep the e_____ from its factory within a_____ limits.

It's _____ that the public should have strong _____ about any t_____ to their safety, but believe me, their fears in this case are completely groundless.

country	hazardous	image
countryside	noxious	press release
environment	poisonous	pressure group
landscape	toxic	
nature		confidence
surroundings	compensation	faith
	damage	feeling
acceptable	effluent	trust
natural	fumes	
	harm	
conservation	pollution	
conservationist	risk	
	threat	
contaminate	waste	
poison		
pollute		

101

ON THE AIR: A DANGEROUS ENCOUNTER

Read or listen to this dialogue.

Lars Laurensen is being interviewed on a local radio programme about the effect of his factory on the environment. The interviewer is Susan Brown.

Susan Mr Laurensen, we all know that Newsea Chemicals is a subsidiary of International Carbonide. Who do you actually take your orders from?

Lars Well, it's not quite as simple as that. It depends what you mean by 'orders'.

Susan Let me put it this way. To stop pollution in Newsea from carbon dust would cost one and a half million pounds...

Lars May I interrupt? I think you've been misinformed. In the three years since my Corporation came to Newsea, we've spent nearly a million pounds on smoke-cleansing equipment. We have removed 94.5 per cent of impurities from the smoke. To remove the remaining 5.5 per cent would simply not be economic.

Susan Ah! So if you *did* spend one and a half million, you'd probably lose your job?

Lars No, I wouldn't go so far as to say that. Of course, if we consistently run at a loss, then I shall lose my job—and so will about five hundred of my fellow citizens in Newsea.

Susan But you'll have a nice job lined up for you in Geneva or somewhere, whereas they'll be unemployed.

Lars I really don't quite see what you're getting at; in fact, your last remark seems to me rather unhelpful. Of course there's no question whatever of the factory closing.

Susan Aren't we rather evading the issue? The fact is that most of the pollution in your area doesn't come from the factory chimneys. It's the carbon dust itself, your main product.

Lars I'm afraid I can't altogether accept that. It's only one among a range of products—all of them vital to a modern industrial society.

Susan All right then, let's turn to another source of anxiety for your fellow citizens. Project 73: isn't it a fact that this is emitting dangerous lead compounds and that you yourself would like it moved to a less populated area?

Lars That's a very complex question. I'd like to re-phrase it if I may—

Susan We're running out of time, Mr Laurensen. Is Project 73 dangerous?

Lars No—and we shall continue to monitor lead levels in the environment as an additional safety check.

1 Listen again and find as many expressions as possible which are used to deal with awkward questions.
2 Practise the expressions recorded after the dialogue on the tape.
3 With the following check-list to help you, do the role-playing exercise.

DEALING WITH AWKWARD QUESTIONS

It's not quite as simple as that.
It depends what you mean by...
I think you've been misinformed.
I wouldn't go so far as to say that.
I don't quite see what you're getting at.
There's no question whatever of...
The fact is that...
I'm afraid I can't altogether accept that.
That's a very complex question.
I'd like to re-phrase that, if I may.

Role-playing exercise

Representatives of the Residents' Action Committee in Newsea have just heard that two very senior International Carbonide Corporation executives are in town: Ms Ginetti (from Italy) and Mr Hulkonnen (from Finland). The Residents demand, and get, a meeting with them in their hotel. This is the Residents' chance to find out the truth about rumours that Carbonide plan to expand the factory; to close it down; to build a nuclear reactor; to build a by-pass; to import workers from overseas, etc. They also want to know the visitors' attitudes to environmental problems. Unfortunately, the visitors are not willing to give away very much information.

SWINGS AND TRENDS

Excited by the recent outcry against pollution in Newsea, the local newspaper has been doing some investigating. The following article speaks for itself.

ONE THIRD OF NEWSEA RESIDENTS WANT CARBONIDE TO CLOSE

(continued from page 1)

The results of the *Herald Argus* poll may be usefully compared with opinions that were expressed in previous polls. The first was held in 1979, when the closure of Newsea Town Mill was already being considered.

1979 (population 10,570; 5% unemployment)
1. Should Newsea Town Steel Mill close? —
   Yes 17%   No 69%   Don't Know 14%
2. Do you/Does your husband work in the mill?
   Yes 36%   No 64%
3. What will you do if the mill closes? (Those who answered 'yes' to Question 2.)
   Look for another job in Newsea 48%
   Go on the dole 13%   Leave Newsea 33%
   Don't know 6%

When the second poll was held in 1986, Newsea Town Mill had already been closed for three years and Carbonide were negotiating the purchase of the buildings.

1986 (population 8,690; 24% unemployment)
1. Should International Carbonide take over Newsea Town Mill?
   Yes 84%   No 13%   Don't Know 3%
2. Which is the more serious threat to Newsea?
   Unemployment 81%   Pollution 8%
   Don't Know 11%

1991 (population 7,320; 10% unemployment)
1. How long have you lived in Newsea?
   Less than 5 years 18%   5—10 years 9%
   10—15 years 26%   More than 15 years 47%
2. Which is the more serious threat to Newsea?
   Unemployment 46%   Pollution 49%
   Don't Know 5%
3. Should ICC close its factory at Newsea?
   Yes 31%   No 39%   Don't Know 30%

Consider the figures and answer these questions:

1. How many of the 500 workers at Newsea Chemicals are, probably, newcomers to the town?

2. Which percentages suggest the biggest swing between one poll and another?

3. What trends appear in these figures that would either encourage or discourage (a) the Residents' Action Committee (b) Lars Laurensen?

THE RIGHT WORDS IN THE RIGHT PLACE

Maggie Fulton, the Chairman of the Residents' Action Committee, is a very effective public speaker. When she is going to make a speech about a matter of public concern, she usually takes with her a few press cuttings, a photograph, a letter or a pamphlet which will remind her of the points she wants to make. Below, you can see some of the materials she took to the protest meeting in the Newsea Community Hall (see Casebook). The first extract is part of a Public Relations handout written by Lars Laurensen. The headlines are all cut from local newspapers during the past twelve months.

Finally, may we remind you of some of the benefits which the International Carbonide Corporation can claim to have brought to Newsea:

- The reinstatement of an historic factory building, of architectural distinction, which might have become derelict.
- The creation of jobs for some 500 people, nearly all of them recruited in Newsea or its immediate neighbourhood.
- A renewed sense of community spirit and optimism for the future backed by hard cash. Subsidies have been provided to local choral societies, rugby football teams, schools, and the Newsea Jubilee Leisure Centre.

Below you can see how Maggie Fulton began this section of her speech. Continue writing it for her, in the same way, using the PR handout and the newspaper headlines.

Carbonide claim to have brought all sorts of benefits to Newsea; for example, they say they've rescued a factory building that ought to be preserved.

---

30 TONS PER YEAR!
CARBON DUST POLLUTION PER SQUARE KILOMETRE MEASURED BY CAMBRIDGE SCIENTISTS

NEWSEA: VILLAGE OF THE DAMNED
Japanese scientist's warning of lead in air, rivers, soil

Second fatal accident in Newsea
11-YR-OLD KILLED BY CARBONIDE TRUCK

WRITTEN ASSIGNMENT

Not surprisingly, rumours of events in Newsea have come to the ears of the Directors of International Carbonide in their well-appointed central office in Brussels. Lars Laurensen is not much astonished to receive a request for a report on the situation.

> After the final group meeting has decided what action should be taken, write Laurensen's report to the Board. It should not contain information that is familiar to the Directors already, but it should say why there is opposition to Newsea Chemicals, where the opposition comes from, and how the situation is being handled.

STEP BY STEP

Keep this report short and crisp. If you let it get out of control, you will try to cover too much ground. Even the title should be brief; the name of the factory, by itself, is probably sufficient.

The terms of reference should be stated very simply. Think along these lines:

> ... problems that have appeared in the field of public relations ...
>
> ... difficulties that have arisen between the factory and its neighbourhood ...
>
> ... conflicts that have developed due to local opposition to the factory ...

Don't start analysing these problems or conflicts at this stage.

There will be no section on *Procedure*, because the report contains only what you already know. However, a brief introduction to the history of Newsea Chemicals may be useful. The vital facts are: the date of the company's formation; its location in Newsea; your presence as Manager throughout.

THE FINDINGS

Having cleared the ground, and reminded your Directors of what they ought to know, but have probably forgotten, you can get down to the real business of the report. You have a lot of bits of information of many different sorts; you must find some way to classify these—to write a small number of main headings under which all your bits of information can be logically arranged.

One possible arrangement, or set of headings, would be:

> *The causes of complaint* (or *The reasons for pollution*)
> *The nature of the opposition* (or *Protests from the community*)
> *The management's proposed course of action*

Alternatively, you may prefer to develop the historical approach, perhaps on these lines:

> *Reasons for the location of Newsea Chemicals*
> *Efforts to build up good relations with the local community*
> *The rise of opposition*
> *The nature of complaints against Newsea Chemicals*
> *Proposed course of action*

Both these approaches are valid; both lead to totally different reports. Other ways of setting about the report can be found. For instance, you may decide that the environmental problems which Newsea Chemicals is alleged to be causing (because of carbon dust; heavy lorries; lead from Project 73) are so different that each requires a separate section of the report to itself.

Remember, too, that Newsea Chemicals has some friends. Many people in Newsea want the factory to keep on working; they may well be a 'silent majority'.

CONCLUSIONS

You must attempt an analysis of the parties and interests that are ranged against you, and their probable strength. You will have to do some inventing here, but don't invent more than you have to. The opposition may be united or it may not; it may include angry housewives, property owners worried about the value of their investments, conservationists (both moderate and extremist), politicians, and even unemployed local young people who are just bored.

Finally, say what action you have decided to take. No recommendations were asked for.

Alternative assignment

Imagine that you are Michael Richards, living in Newsea. You strongly support the work of Newsea Chemicals and you think for various reasons, that the firm must not be closed down, moved, or forced to operate under unnecessary difficulties. Write a letter for publication in the local newspaper putting your point of view.

HEARD IN THE LOCAL NEWSPAPER OFFICE

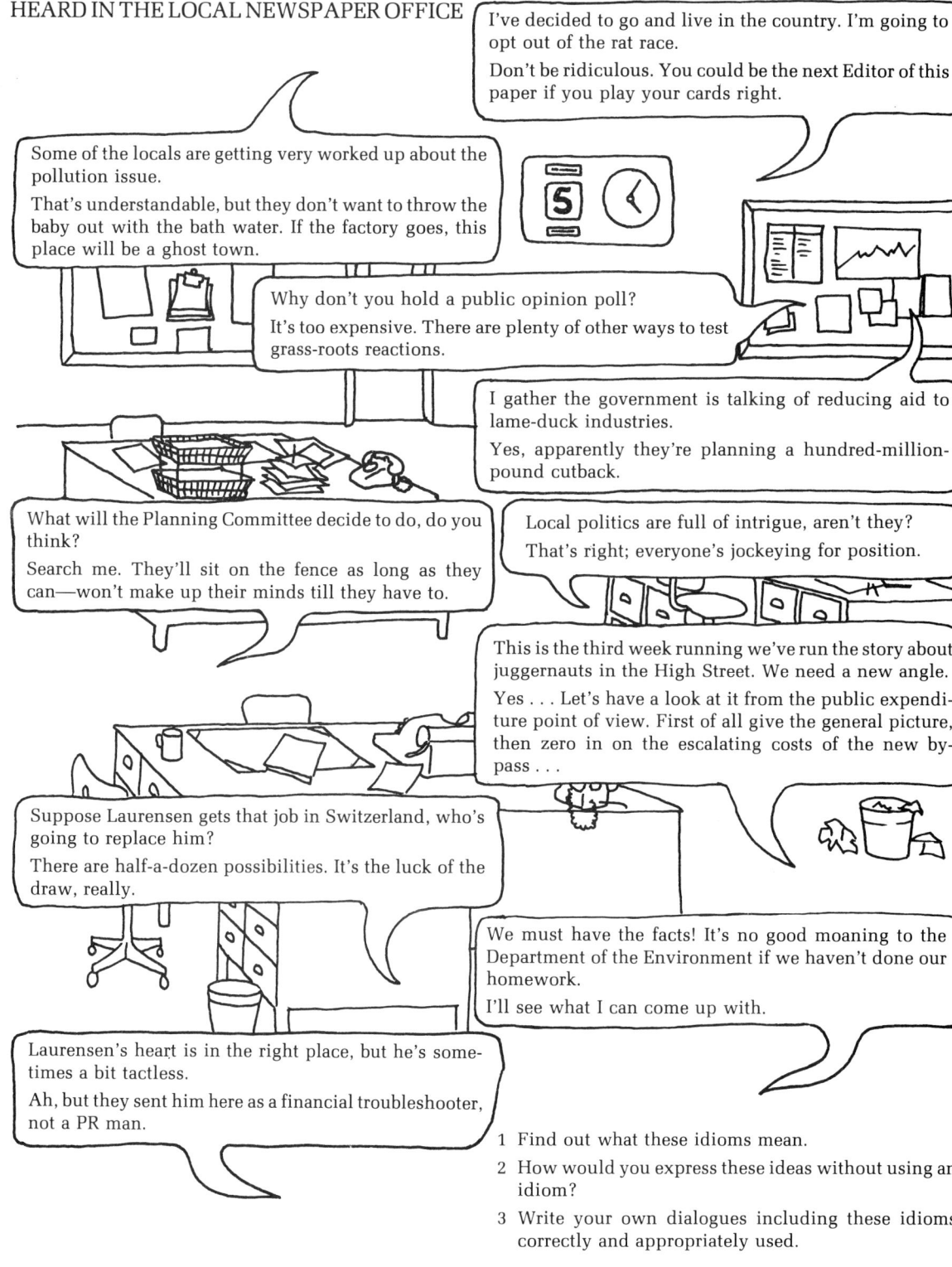

I've decided to go and live in the country. I'm going to opt out of the rat race.
Don't be ridiculous. You could be the next Editor of this paper if you play your cards right.

Some of the locals are getting very worked up about the pollution issue.
That's understandable, but they don't want to throw the baby out with the bath water. If the factory goes, this place will be a ghost town.

Why don't you hold a public opinion poll?
It's too expensive. There are plenty of other ways to test grass-roots reactions.

I gather the government is talking of reducing aid to lame-duck industries.
Yes, apparently they're planning a hundred-million-pound cutback.

What will the Planning Committee decide to do, do you think?
Search me. They'll sit on the fence as long as they can—won't make up their minds till they have to.

Local politics are full of intrigue, aren't they?
That's right; everyone's jockeying for position.

This is the third week running we've run the story about juggernauts in the High Street. We need a new angle.
Yes ... Let's have a look at it from the public expenditure point of view. First of all give the general picture, then zero in on the escalating costs of the new by-pass ...

Suppose Laurensen gets that job in Switzerland, who's going to replace him?
There are half-a-dozen possibilities. It's the luck of the draw, really.

We must have the facts! It's no good moaning to the Department of the Environment if we haven't done our homework.
I'll see what I can come up with.

Laurensen's heart is in the right place, but he's sometimes a bit tactless.
Ah, but they sent him here as a financial troubleshooter, not a PR man.

1. Find out what these idioms mean.
2. How would you express these ideas without using an idiom?
3. Write your own dialogues including these idioms correctly and appropriately used.

AFJUZ

UNDERSTANDING THE CASE

Read the case study in the Casebook and answer these questions.

1. If you are marketing a product such as citrus fruit, why is it important to make housewives familiar with the brand name?
2. Why is it difficult to do this?
3. What is a marketing board? Who finances, and who benefits from the board described in this case study?
4. Why did Chamass first contact Ms Spandrel?
5. Why does Chamass feel that he has been let down?
6. Why has the problem of marketing AFJUZ oranges become especially urgent?
7. El-Din suggests that the oranges should be sold well below cost price, undercutting rivals by a large margin. Why is this proposal unacceptable?
8. Why have Clutton & Cummings concentrated on selling to wholesalers and caterers? What is the disadvantage of relying on this sector of the market?
9. 'With twice as much money, we could make four times as much impact.' (Clutton & Cummings's Advertising Manager.) Could there be any truth in this remark?
10. When you decide how to spend AFJUZ's advertising budget, what factors will influence you most?

VOCABULARY Brands, products and types

Jenny Coleman, one of Clutton & Cummings's bright young marketing executives, talks about some of the difficulties of her job. Fill in the gaps in her remarks by taking words from the box below.

Jenny Marketing agricultural p_____ is never very easy, not even when you're working for a big organization and the p_____ is already up among the _____ leaders. Citrus fruit (oranges, lemons, that _____ of thing) is a(n) _____ good example of the problem.

For a start, the market is _____. No one can eat more than a(n) _____ amount of fruit. It's one of the _____ on every housewife's shopping list, but most people can't tell one _____ of orange from another. So they either take what the greengrocer gives them, or else they look for a _____ n_____ that they're familiar with.

Admittedly, we sell a lot of un_____ oranges to supermarkets and food chains who distribute them under their own _____. But this doesn't really help the citrus _____ who want their fruit to be sold under their _____ brand name.

That's one reason, of course, why we often wrap i_____ oranges in tissue paper, or stamp AFJUZ on the orange itself. As long as the name is a _____ t_____, no one else can use it.

What do I think of AFJUZ? Well, they're just oranges. They're nice, but they're nothing s_____.

brand	goods	certain
brand name	item	especial(ly)
(un)branded	produce	individual(ly)
label	producer	limit
registered	product	limited
trademark	production	own
		particular(ly)
	kind	peculiar
	sort	special(ly)
	type	

AN AGENT DEFENDS HIS RECORD

Read or listen to the dialogue.

Abdul Chamass is visiting the Citrus Marketing Board's London agent. The General Manager, James Lethbridge, is defending his company's rather disappointing record.

Chamass It's no secret, James, that we're unhappy with the way things are going.

Lethbridge I understand that, but it's not our fault that things haven't gone as well as we'd all expected. It takes time—and patience—to get a brand established, especially when the competition's so powerful and highly organized.

Chamass I know all that, but Helen Spandrel was sure we'd have three per cent of the market by now. In fact, of course, we're nowhere near the target.

Lethbridge We've got some way to go yet, it's true. Mind you, we've done very well with the hotels and catering trade. They've given us something to build on.

El-Din There's one thing you can't deny, James. You haven't reached the housewife at all. She's the person who buys most of the oranges sold in this country.

Lethbridge I accept that. The question is, why haven't we done better in the grocery shops, the stores and the supermarkets? One of our problems is that we can't afford to advertise. You know I'm not the kind of person who makes excuses, but it's a fact we need a much bigger advertising budget. If we're going to get the AFJUZ brand across to the public and trade, we need to spend more money.

Chamass You may well have a point there. Actually, we're looking hard at our commitments now. We may be able to increase the budget for sales promotion.

Lethbridge That would be very welcome.

Chamass Look, James, there is one thing I want to say to you, and I'm afraid it may not be very pleasant . . .

Lethbridge Oh yes?

Chamass As you know, our agreement's coming up for renewal shortly. Well, we're currently looking at other ways of developing sales over here.

Lethbridge I see . . . So you're going to drop us, are you?

Chamass Don't worry, nothing's been decided. In fact, we're keeping an open mind at present. We know marketing AFJUZ oranges over here isn't easy. We also realize that Rome wasn't built in a day . . .

1 Listen again and find as many expressions as possible which are used to make excuses or defend poor results.
2 Practise the expressions recorded after the dialogue on the tape.
3 With the following check-list to help you, do the role-playing exercise.

MAKING EXCUSES/EXPLAINING POOR RESULTS

It's not our fault that things haven't gone as well as we'd expected.
It takes time to . . .
Mind you, we've done very well in some areas.
One of our problems is that . . .
I'm not the kind who makes excuses, but . . .
Don't forget, . . .
We're not really to blame if . . .
Let me give you the background to this.

Role-playing exercise

The owner of a London hotel is unhappy about the service he is receiving from the wholesale greengrocers he deals with. Fruit sent to him directly from the company's depot has been arriving in poor condition. Part of each consignment has been unripe or damaged because of bad packing. The reason for this is simple. The packers and loaders at the depot recently asked for a wage increase, but their claim was flatly refused by management. In protest, they are not working as efficiently as they would normally. The General Manager and the London Sales Representative go over to the hotel to try to calm down its owner and the head of the catering services.

LIMITED BUDGET, MAXIMUM IMPACT

Jenny Coleman is a young marketing executive with Clutton & Cummings. She has been given the job of carrying out a one-week intensive promotion campaign on behalf of AFJUZ grapefruit. These grapefruit are smaller and thinner-skinned than English people are accustomed to, but they are juicy and full of sweetness and flavour. Jenny is determined to show what her firm can do. She has a budget of only £1,000, and therefore chooses a small town just outside London as her target area. She collects the following information about the ways in which she may be able to advertise the product:

Target Area: Olchester, Freeshire   Population: 58,270
                                                          Retail fruit outlets: 47

Media and costs   Advertising rates

1 Local press

   West Freeshire Echo   Weekly (Thurs)   Half-page   £240
                              Circulation about 35,000   Full page   £410
                              3,000? in Olchester itself   Two-page
                                                              spread   £780

   Olchester Evening News   Evening (not Sun)   Half-page   £30
                              2,600–3,000 copies   (full week)   £150
                                                            Full page   £60
                                                              (full week)   £300

   Freeshire Advertiser   Weekly   Display ads
                              8,500 copies distributed   10cm x 5cm   £50
                              free to householders   and pro rata

2 Sales literature (printed locally)

   (a) Banners for shop-fronts, etc.   Each   £1
   (b) Wallcharts/posters for shops   Each   £0.50
   (c) Handouts   Per 100   £3.50

3 Hire of double-deck bus (with driver and loudspeaker
   system) to tour area, carry display material and   For one week   £500
   literature etc.

4 Two female merchandisers to accompany bus, distribute
   literature and free grapefruit, etc.   £180

5 Free distribution of grapefruit   Per 100   £10

Consider how Jenny can obtain maximum impact without going over her £1,000 budget.

THE RIGHT WORDS IN THE RIGHT PLACE

Whenever Gamal El-Din visits an AFJUZ sales outlet, he pays particular attention to anything that the owner or manager of the business says to him regarding AFJUZ's marketing methods. So as not to forget these comments, he writes them up in his diary at the end of the day.

> Below are some comments made to Mr El-Din by Mr Phillips, the Manager of a wholesale cash-and-carry store. In the example, you will see the first of the diary entries for this conversation. Write the other diary entries in the same way.

Example

Mr Phillips You know, yesterday I was talking to one of the boys who runs a stall in the market. He told me you lot were developing a new type of grapefruit. How come you haven't told me anything about it?

Diary *Phillips has heard from a business contact about our new grapefruit project. Is surprised we haven't given him any information about it.*

1 Now, what on earth's happening with these lemon cartons? Don't you remember? I told you that a lot of our customers want smaller packages, say, six to eight kilos. They're easy to handle and slip into the back of a van. You fellows come up with a smaller container for lemons, and we'll fill your order book, I promise you.

2 What's wrong with AFJUZ? Well, take your oranges. OK, the quality's marvellous—juicy, easy to peel, and they keep well. But, speaking as a customer, I must say you never know when you're going to get some. We get a consignment one day, then we may not get another for a month or so, then we get a huge pile of them all at once. What a way to do business!

3 Let me tell you something. This morning, I was standing on the escalator in the tube at Liverpool Street station. As I went up, I looked at the advertising panels on the opposite wall. What did I see? 'Sicilian Oranges . . . Sicilian Oranges . . .' Not once but eight times that panel passed before my eyes! Now, that's what AFJUZ should be doing. Hitting the public right between the eyes with its brand name.

WRITTEN ASSIGNMENT

> When the one-week sales campaign is over (see the numeracy exercise), Jenny Coleman has to write a report on it for Mr Cummings. This will help him to decide on a marketing policy for AFJUZ grapefruit in Great Britain—and, he hopes, to persuade AFJUZ to renew the agency agreement. Draft Jenny's report for her.

STARTING

Decide what information you are going to need:

(a) about the town: where is it? how many people live there? what sort of people? where do they shop?

(b) about the methods you used: how did you allocate your budget? how did you test consumer reaction—did you ask people to peel and eat a grapefruit in the street?

(c) about the results: how many grapefruit were sold during the week? did sales rise or fall? what other factors influenced sales—for example, weather, shortage of other fruit, etc? what were wholesale and retail prices—the retail price of a grapefruit is likely to be about 25p? what did consumers and retailers say about AFJUZ grapefruit? how many repeat orders have been placed?

Then decide what recommendations you will make: should AFJUZ grapefruit be launched on a large scale in the UK? regionally or nationally? at a high price or a low one? in small quantities or in bulk? The population of Great Britain is approximately 1,000 times that of Jenny's target area; what sort of budget would be needed for the first year? What features of AFJUZ grapefruit would you draw to people's attention: sweetness, flavour, juiciness, size, price, ease of peeling, long life in storage?

PRESENTATION
(a) The *Title* and *Terms of reference* should give you no difficulty. The *Procedures* are longer and more complex than usual: you need to say exactly how your £1,000 was spent, and how you collected information about the results of your campaign.
(b) Present your *Findings* in short paragraphs or sub-paragraphs. You will find headings useful here—e.g. *Sales*; *Consumer reaction*; *Repeat orders*; etc.
(c) Your *Conclusions* and *Recommendations* are crucial! You must be
- precise: how many grapefruit should Clutton & Cummings expect to sell per week for the first year?
- cautious: make it clear that 'We can meet this sales target only if . . .'

Alternative assignment

You own and manage a greengrocer's shop near London. You saw the AFJUZ grapefruit campaign from the retailer's point of view. You are keen to sell AFJUZ produce and you have definite ideas of your own about how Clutton & Cummings should set about marketing it. Write to the Marketing Manager and outline your criticisms of the grapefruit campaign and your suggestions for the future.

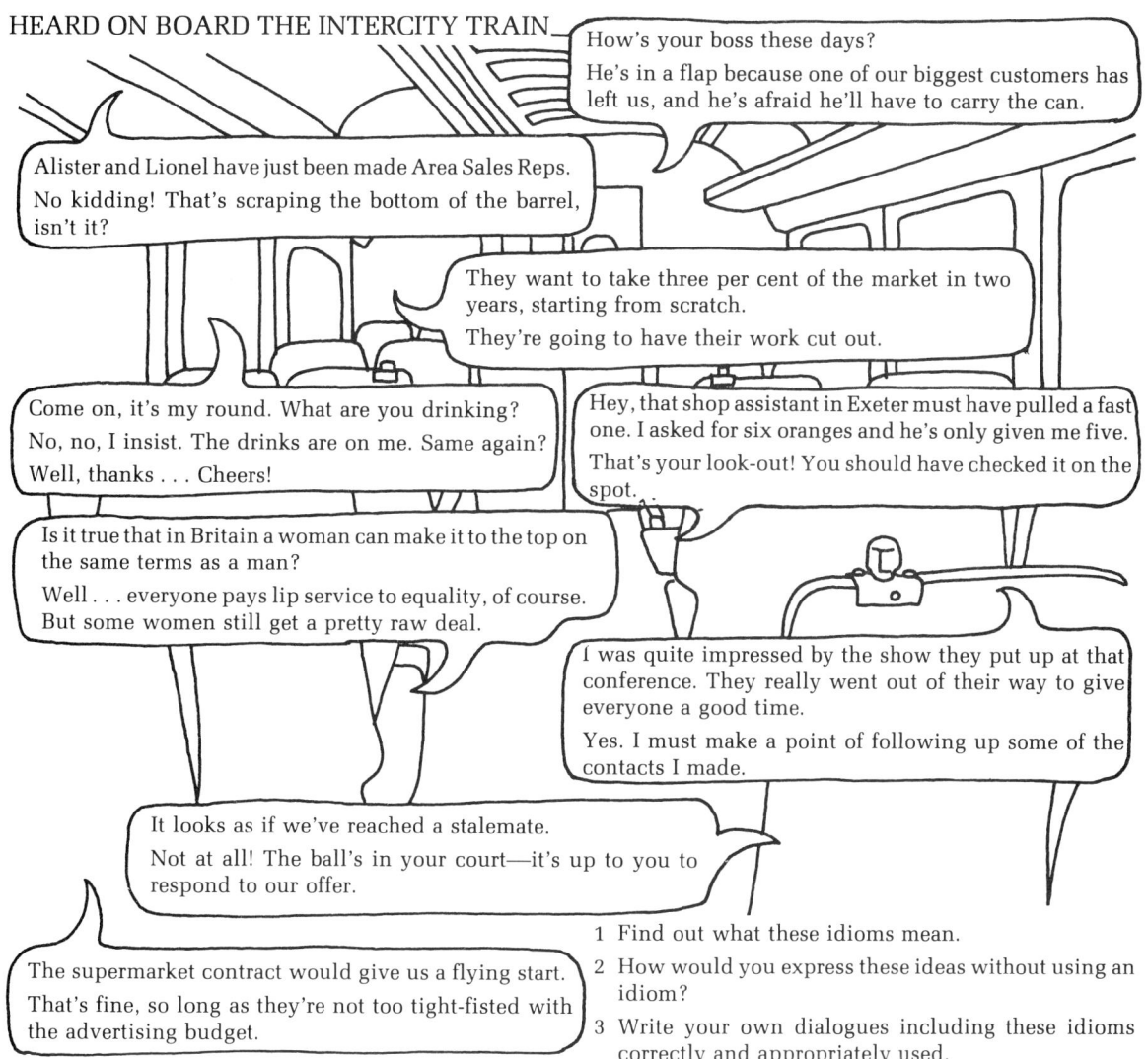

HEARD ON BOARD THE INTERCITY TRAIN

How's your boss these days?
He's in a flap because one of our biggest customers has left us, and he's afraid he'll have to carry the can.

Alister and Lionel have just been made Area Sales Reps.
No kidding! That's scraping the bottom of the barrel, isn't it?

They want to take three per cent of the market in two years, starting from scratch.
They're going to have their work cut out.

Come on, it's my round. What are you drinking?
No, no, I insist. The drinks are on me. Same again?
Well, thanks . . . Cheers!

Hey, that shop assistant in Exeter must have pulled a fast one. I asked for six oranges and he's only given me five.
That's your look-out! You should have checked it on the spot.

Is it true that in Britain a woman can make it to the top on the same terms as a man?
Well . . . everyone pays lip service to equality, of course. But some women still get a pretty raw deal.

I was quite impressed by the show they put up at that conference. They really went out of their way to give everyone a good time.
Yes. I must make a point of following up some of the contacts I made.

It looks as if we've reached a stalemate.
Not at all! The ball's in your court—it's up to you to respond to our offer.

The supermarket contract would give us a flying start.
That's fine, so long as they're not too tight-fisted with the advertising budget.

1 Find out what these idioms mean.
2 How would you express these ideas without using an idiom?
3 Write your own dialogues including these idioms correctly and appropriately used.

KYOSEC

UNDERSTANDING THE CASE
Read the case study in the Casebook and answer these questions.

1 What role does Brismel Investments play in the management of Kyoung-Sung Electrical?
2 Why is high profitability important for Kyoung-Sung?
3 What can Kyoung-Sung produce that their competitors have so far not been able to make?
4 Why is a recording on a compact cassette more attractive than the same recording on a standard TV cassette?
5 Why is it important for a company like Kyoung-Sung to keep on marketing new inventions and new models?
6 Why is it important for them to be able to meet large orders quickly?
7 Why are their production plans threatened?
8 In the short term (say, the next twelve to eighteen months), which matters more for Kyoung-Sung: their profits or their reputation?
9 Why can't the problem of the colour TV tubes simply be handed over to the Head of Production for him to solve?
10 'You're going to have to gamble on something,' (Robert Lee). What is at stake for Kyoung-Sung in adopting any one of the four options proposed?

VOCABULARY Makes, models and features

Robert Lee, Assistant Brand Manager for Kyosec products, gets very enthusiastic when he talks about his firm's range. Fill in the gaps in his remarks by taking words from the box below.

Lee Kyosec is only one among many _____s of home entertainment _____, but believe me, we're the pace-setters. Take our new CVC 90, for instance. Advance _____s are the highest for any m_____ that we've ever produced.

The technical s_____ is quite remarkable. I've never seen a _____ of this size with so many of the f_____s you'd normally only find on a full-size _____. For instance, there's no _____ to tune it exactly to the channel you want: it's got a _____ which _____s to the incoming signal and adjusts the tuner automatically.

The trouble is going to be to _____ the _____ that we're expecting. We have a(n) _____ to our dealers all over the world to _____ them with the goods their customers _____. But our dealers are under no _____ to us. There are no exclusive agreements. So keeping up with our production schedules isn't just desirable; it's an absolute _____.

I guess the CVC 90 isn't exactly easy to make. Each _____ has over three thousand five hundred separate _____s. Of course, you'll be able to buy a full range of _____ to use with it: extension speakers, stereo microphones, maybe even a miniaturized TV camera. Think what a g_____t like that could do for home movies!

brand	accessory	answer
make	component	fulfil
maker	feature	meet
manufacturer	spare (part)	respond
		supply
model	commitment	
outfit	demand	oblige
set	necessity	require
unit	need	specify
	obligation	want
device	order	
equipment	requirement	
gadget	specification	
machine		
machinery		

BRAINSTORMING SESSION

Read or listen to the dialogue.

Mr Lee, Mrs Noya, Mr Chun and Mr Stansfield are in Mr Chun's office in Masan, South Korea. They are trying to work out what to do about the non-delivery of the colour TV tubes for the new CVC 90.

Lee ... My suggestion would be to bring forward the Starstripe.

Noya Yes—as long as the design engineers are satisfied with it. It's not worth marketing unless it's absolutely OK.

Lee I know the designers want more time, but you're going to have to gamble on something.

Chun Not unless all else fails—and even then only on condition that the market report is favourable.

Stansfield Oh, we know the report will be favourable all right—that is, if the consultants ever get around to writing it.

Lee That's a point. They've been at it for six months now. We commissioned them on the understanding that they could do a rush job.

Noya Our consultants' report in South America was very favourable—and very punctual. The only proviso they made for the success of the CVC 90 was that there should be ample stocks on retailers' shelves from the word go! So now what am I going to say to my people in Brazil? They've placed big orders—conditional on early delivery! And they want colour sets.

Stansfield All the same, you must admit that even with black and white the CVC 90 is still an attractive proposition.

Noya Surely you could manufacture these tubes yourselves!

Chun As long as your company is prepared to put up fifty million dollars for a new factory, yes ... and provided, of course, that you can wait six months while we build it.

Lee Yes, why not? If you could only persuade Brismel Investments to advance the money!

Stansfield Not much chance of that, I'm afraid. Only if we had a controlling interest in the company would we consider such massive investment ... and in any case, as foreign investors, we're only allowed to hold up to a certain percentage of the equity.

Chun So you see, we're working under a number of constraints.

Lee Shortage of capital is always a limiting factor ...

Chun Shall we adjourn for lunch? We can continue this discussion afterwards—that is, if you're free this afternoon ...

1 Listen again and find as many expressions as possible which are used to talk about the conditions necessary to allow certain things to happen.

2 Practise the expressions recorded after the dialogue on the tape.

3 With the following check-list to help you, do the role-playing exercise.

MAKING CONDITIONS

We could do it, as long as ...
It's not worth ——ing unless ...
I won't do it unless all else fails.
Even then, I'll only do it on condition that ...
We did it on the understanding that ...
The only proviso was that ...
They've agreed—conditional on ...
If you could only ...
Provided you can ..., we can ...
Only if ..., would we ...

Role-playing exercise

Mr Rao and M. Dalais are partners in an import business on the island of Mauritius. They are keen to become sole agents for Kyosec products on the island. The nearest Kyoung-Sung branch office is in Bombay, and after an exchange of letters the two of them go there to discuss the terms of the agency. Both parties in the negotiations—the two men from Mauritius and the representatives of Kyoung-Sung—are determined to impose conditions which are as favourable as possible for themselves.

SPECIFICATIONS

Back in 1988, Mr James Brewster ran a hi-fi business in London. A lot of his customers were interested in portable TV/radio/cassette recorders, which were still fairly recent innovations. Below, you can see pictures and brief technical specifications of two very successful sets reproduced from the manufacturer's publicity material of that year.

Compare the features and specification of each set, assuming that it is still 1988 and that these are the current models and prices. What advice would you give to the following people on which set to buy?

1. A family which travels a lot with teenage children who are crazy about sport and pop music.
2. A young man who likes to impress his friends by always having the latest and most expensive toy.
3. A middle-aged housewife who wants to follow an Open University course involving radio and TV programmes.
4. A school that wants to buy a dozen sets for use with small groups of pupils.
5. A long-stay patient in a hospital ward.

K 50

5" Tube Portable Monochrome Television with 3 Band Radio and Cassette Recorder. Approx picture diagonal $4\frac{3}{4}$"

The complete portable entertainment centre. TV, FM/LW/MW radio and cassette recorder all-in-one. Ideal for caravaning, camping and boating. Powerful high quality output. Cassette recorder includes Review/cue, auto-stop, pause, 3-digit counter and record/tuning/battery level meter. Dial illumination. Carrying support handle. Mains lead/C60 Cassette/S/N Plug/Light shelter hood/12V Car battery lead.

Audio Output: 2W (max) / Frequency Range: UHF channels 21-68 TV 625 lines, FM band 87.5-103 MHz, MW 530-1605 kHz, LW 150-350 kHz / Size: (WHD) 420 x 130 x 320mm approx. / Approx. Av. Weight: 7 kg (15.4lbs) including batteries / Power Supply: 240V AC mains, 12V car battery (external socket), 15V (UM 1G x 10) batteries.

rrp £194

P 57

12" Tube Transportable Monochrome Television with 3 Band Radio and Cassette Recorder. Approx picture picture diagonal $11\frac{1}{2}$"

The ultimate compact home transportable with TV, FM/LW/MW radio and cassette recorder all-in-one. All the many features you would expect from HITACHI plus top quality electronics, high quality picture, attractive design and reliability. TV auto-search and manual tuning. Complete specification cassette recorder including built-in microphone and tape counter. Powerful output from large speaker. Mains car battery operation. Built-in radio aerial and external TV socket.

Audio Output: 2W (max) / Frequency Range: UHF channels 21-68 TV 625 lines, FM band 88-108 MHz, LW 150-350 KHz MW 530-1605 kHz / Size: (WHD) 510 x 330 x 290mm approx / Approx. Av. Weight: 9.2 kg Power Supply: 240V AC mains, 12V DC car battery / Accessories: Car Battery lead, earphone, cassette tape, erase plug.

rrp £208

rrp = recommended retail price

THE RIGHT WORDS IN THE RIGHT PLACE

Alec Stansfield, of Brismel Investments, is always being asked for free advice—not least by his aged Aunt Matilda. Matilda came to Australia years ago with a portfolio full of shares in British companies which she resolutely refuses to sell. Among what she considers to be her blue-chip investments is a block of 5,000 shares in Goody's Department Stores Ltd, of London. At the moment, Goody's is the object of a takeover battle, with two companies—Ernesto and Rainfields—trying to persuade shareholders to sell their holdings. Aunt Matilda recently clipped from a British newspaper the advertisement which you see below. She sent it to her nephew Alec with a request that he should 'explain what on earth it means, in language I can understand'.

Below, you will see how Alec Stansfield dealt with the first part of Goody's advertisement. Continue his letter for him. It should be much shorter than the advertisement, as well as simpler. He is not giving any advice at this stage; he is simply explaining to his aunt what each paragraph of the advertisement means.

Example

As you probably know, there's a firm called Ernesto who want to buy 65 per cent of all Goody's ordinary shares—no doubt you've received details of their offer. They're ready to pay £8.75 per share.

But there's another company, Rainfields, . . .

GOODY'S DEPARTMENT STORES (LONDON) LTD

Extracts from the Directors' Circular
dated 20 September 1990

1 This Circular is issued in connection with the offer dated 15 September 1990 by Ernesto & Co Ltd as amended on 17 September 1990, to holders of ordinary shares in Goody's Stores, to acquire 10,500,000 ordinary shares of Goody's (65% control) at a price of £8.75 per share.

2 Reference is also made to the Rainfields offer dated 29 August 1990, and to the Directors' Circular with respect to that offer dated 6 September 1990, in which the Directors recommended that shareholders prepared to recognise the prospects of Goody's Stores over the next few years should not accept the offer. The Rainfields offer was announced on 9 September 1990, and the offer is now for 75% of Goody's shares at a price of £7.95 payable in cash. It is no longer conditional upon the deposit of any minimum number of shares and the expiry date has been extended to 28 September 1990.

3 The Directors have concluded on the basis of advice from the Company's financial advisors that the values of the Ernesto and Rainfields offers per Goody's share are now approximately equal. However, the Ernesto offer is conditional upon Ernesto's obtaining 55% of the outstanding shares. There is therefore a possibility that sufficient shares may be tendered under the Rainfields offer to make it impossible for Ernesto to secure 55% of the shares.

4 In addition, Ernesto's current financial structure, with its present leverage, could have an adverse effect on the future ability of Goody's to finance its long-term development programme and to achieve the earnings projection set out in the Directors' Circular of 6 September 1990.

5 The Board of Goody's has been advised by its financial advisors that, in view of the substantial premium of both offers over the pre-offer market price (£6.05), many shareholders will wish to accept one of the offers. The advisors have also stated that some major shareholders will very likely accept the unconditional Rainfields offer, and thus will be assured that at least 75% of their shares will be purchased under the offer.

6 In all these circumstances, the Directors recommend, in the absence of any further amendments to either offer, that shareholders should accept the Rainfields offer rather than the Ernesto offer. It is suggested that shareholders should deliver their shares to their financial agents with instructions not to deposit until close to the deadline for acceptance of the Rainfields offer so that they will retain their options in case there are further developments.

WRITTEN ASSIGNMENT

Although there has been no official announcement of the CVC 90 (except as part of test marketing exercises), news of it has spread rapidly and it is creating a great deal of interest. When Dong-A, known to be a Kyoung-Sung supplier and sub-contractor, goes into liquidation, the flames of rumour are fanned higher than ever. Indeed, the words in the case study ('Who will make colour picture tubes for Kyoung-Sung's miracle baby now?') are actually a quotation from an article in an Australian business journal.

> In the hope of silencing some of the more extravagant stories that are going around, Robert Lee asks Kyoung-Sung's Public Relations Manager to issue a press release giving enough of the truth to satisfy most people's curiosity. Write a suitable press release for this rather delicate situation.

FORMAL REASSURANCE

The press release should aim, above all, at reassuring everyone—dealers and potential customers in particular. At the same time, it must sound convincing. Any attempt to 'flannel'—that is, to hide the truth or to make soothing noises without giving hard facts—will be detected at once by the reporters and editors who will work up the document into tomorrow's story.

Begin by being disarmingly frank.

As everyone knows/It is common knowledge that Dong-A, one of our principal suppliers/a major supplier of components to our company/with whom KS had placed substantial contracts for the supply of parts, has gone into liquidation.

This puts us in a difficult situation.
This confronts KS with considerable difficulties.
As a result, KS now faces . . .
KS finds itself in a tricky situation/faced with many problems.

Having made this general statement, now be more precise:

In particular, we are now without supplies of . . ./the company finds itself unexpectedly short of . . .
The most serious of these difficulties is that we are left with only six weeks' stock of . . ./supplies of . . . have dried up.

Now show some sympathy for all your frustrated distributors and would-be customers:

This naturally creates serious problems for our customers.
This in turn obviously/inevitably makes it difficult/impossible for our customers to know when to expect delivery of certain products.
Special anxiety has been expressed/Many customers are particularly worried about supplies of KS's amazing new CVC 90.

Say very briefly what the CVC 90 is and what it does —why it is so exceptional: a major technological breakthrough—a product that will sweep the home entertainment market.

Explain that colour tubes are the problem, but that KS has six weeks' supply in hand. Say that the company is taking vigorous steps to find alternative sources of these tubes and is confident of maintaining planned levels of production. Orders may be slightly delayed but will be dealt with in strict rotation.

Properly handled, this press release should read more like an advertisement than an apology. In fact, it should not sound like an apology at all.

Alternative assignment

Production delays or not, the CVC 90 will appear on the market sometime. Sales literature is already being written for it, in many languages. Draft all—or part—of a leaflet in English, drawing attention to the CVC 90's many attractive features and emphasizing its ability to record up to two hours of colour TV and stereo sound on one compact cassette.

HEARD IN THE EXECUTIVE CAR PARK

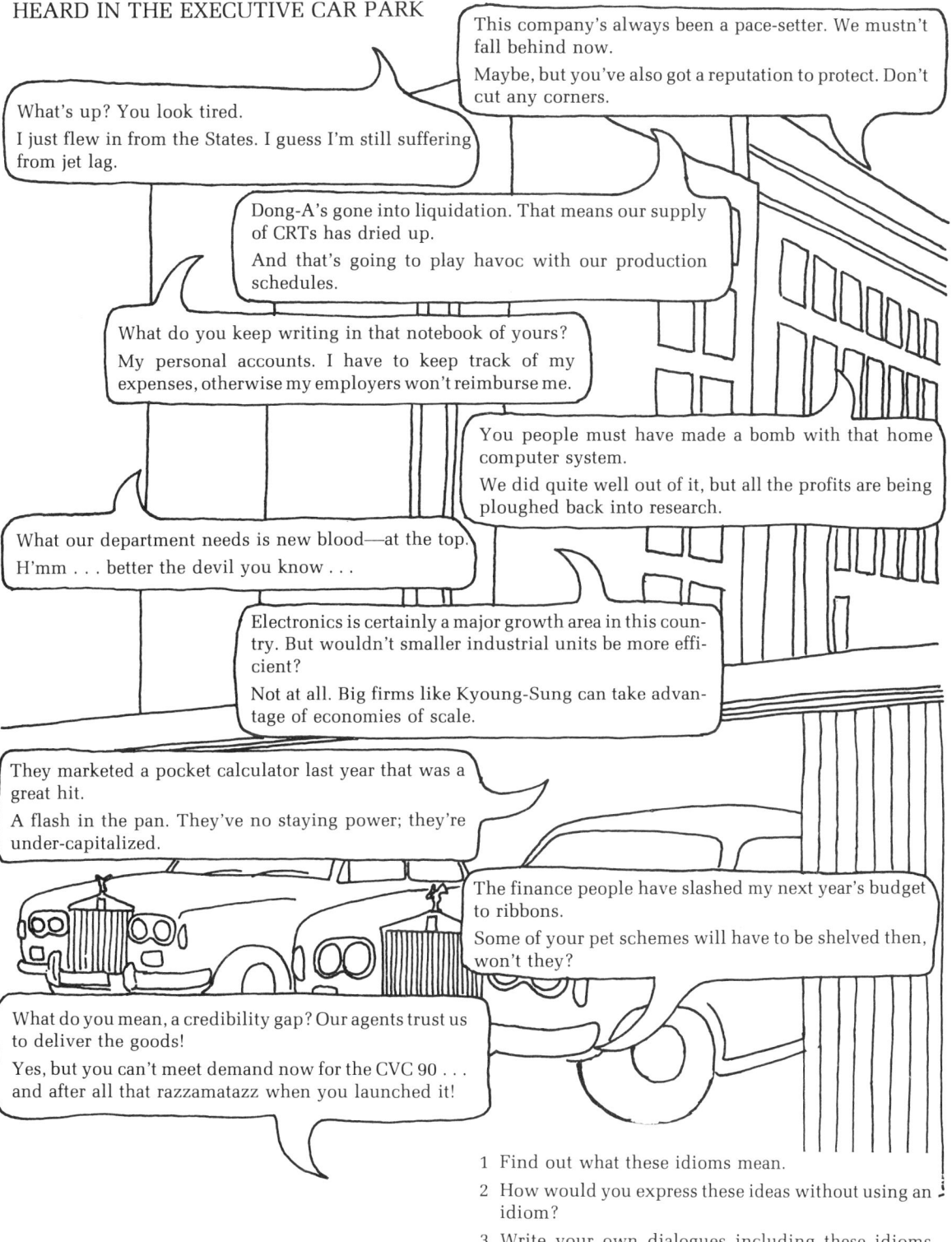

This company's always been a pace-setter. We mustn't fall behind now.
Maybe, but you've also got a reputation to protect. Don't cut any corners.

What's up? You look tired.
I just flew in from the States. I guess I'm still suffering from jet lag.

Dong-A's gone into liquidation. That means our supply of CRTs has dried up.
And that's going to play havoc with our production schedules.

What do you keep writing in that notebook of yours?
My personal accounts. I have to keep track of my expenses, otherwise my employers won't reimburse me.

You people must have made a bomb with that home computer system.
We did quite well out of it, but all the profits are being ploughed back into research.

What our department needs is new blood—at the top.
H'mm . . . better the devil you know . . .

Electronics is certainly a major growth area in this country. But wouldn't smaller industrial units be more efficient?
Not at all. Big firms like Kyoung-Sung can take advantage of economies of scale.

They marketed a pocket calculator last year that was a great hit.
A flash in the pan. They've no staying power; they're under-capitalized.

The finance people have slashed my next year's budget to ribbons.
Some of your pet schemes will have to be shelved then, won't they?

What do you mean, a credibility gap? Our agents trust us to deliver the goods!
Yes, but you can't meet demand now for the CVC 90 . . . and after all that razzamatazz when you launched it!

1. Find out what these idioms mean.
2. How would you express these ideas without using an idiom?
3. Write your own dialogues including these idioms correctly and appropriately used.

APPENDIX: EXAMPLES OF BUSINESS WRITING

SECTION 1: A BUSINESS LETTER

UNIVERSAL FURNITURE & FITTINGS LTD
24-26 COLLIERS WOOD BROADWAY · LONDON SE16   TELEPHONE 01-970 2987

Dudley Morris Esq.   30 April 1990
Chief Purchasing Officer
University of Gatham
Horswick   Your ref.: DM/pjb
Freeshire   Our ref.: bmp/618

Dear Mr Morris

Thank you for your enquiry of 23 April. We enclose a number of leaflets giving details of contract furniture which we believe may meet your requirements, if you can accept a longer delivery date than your letter suggests.

We would particularly draw your attention to a most unusual special offer: 50 club armchairs and 10 matching sofas, luxuriously upholstered in black leather. Although second-hand, these were constructed regardless of cost and will last a lifetime. Full details are enclosed, and we must emphasize that we can offer immediate delivery of these items.

We shall of course be very pleased to send you any further information you may require, and would be glad to welcome you at our showrooms.

Yours sincerely

B.M. Pepper

B.M. Pepper
Sales Manager

NOTES ON THE BUSINESS LETTER
(Based on CHAIRS)

This document, like the three that follow it, illustrates some of the basic conventions of business writing in English. These conventions are intended to make documents easier to write and to read. In the course of your career, however, you will come across plenty of documents in which the conventions are changed or disregarded altogether. The contents and tone of your communication are always, in the end, more important than the conventions of layout or style.

LAYOUT

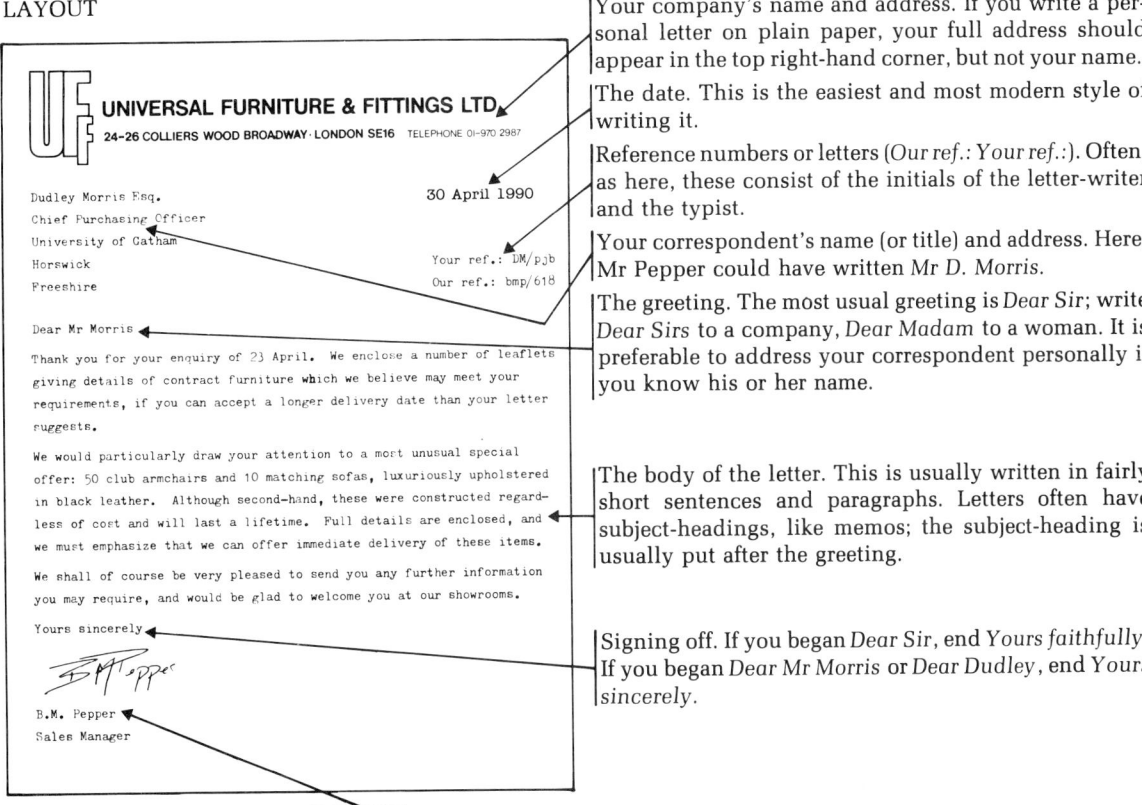

Your company's name and address. If you write a personal letter on plain paper, your full address should appear in the top right-hand corner, but not your name.

The date. This is the easiest and most modern style of writing it.

Reference numbers or letters (*Our ref.: Your ref.:*). Often, as here, these consist of the initials of the letter-writer and the typist.

Your correspondent's name (or title) and address. Here, Mr Pepper could have written *Mr D. Morris*.

The greeting. The most usual greeting is *Dear Sir*; write *Dear Sirs* to a company, *Dear Madam* to a woman. It is preferable to address your correspondent personally if you know his or her name.

The body of the letter. This is usually written in fairly short sentences and paragraphs. Letters often have subject-headings, like memos; the subject-heading is usually put after the greeting.

Signing off. If you began *Dear Sir*, end *Yours faithfully*. If you began *Dear Mr Morris* or *Dear Dudley*, end *Yours sincerely*.

Signature, name and job title. These together are called the 'signature block'.

LANGUAGE AND STYLE

All business documents should be written as clearly and simply as possible, although, in real life, many are not. Avoid elaborate sentence constructions and unnecessarily long words. You should write formally, but you need not be impersonal; you can use *I* and *you* at any time. Avoid using short forms of verbs; for example, write *I do not*, rather than *I don't*.

SECTION 2: AN INTER-OFFICE MEMO

HI-FLITE STORES LTD   MEMORANDUM

From Transport Manager   **To** Loading Bay Supervisor

Date 30 April 1990

Subject <u>Handling of furniture by untrained staff</u>

1 It has come to my notice that in several recent instances furniture has been damaged in the Loading Bay because of careless handling by untrained or inexperienced personnel.

2 Kindly ensure that in future all porters are properly supervised at all times and that adequate means are used to prevent damage to furniture after it has left the sales floor. All items leave the showroom in perfect condition, and must be delivered in the same condition to the customer.

3 I must comment once again on the unsatisfactory relationship that appears to exist between porters and lorry crews. I appreciate the difficulties that these staff face, but I do not believe they are insuperable, given good leadership. I shall appreciate your goodwill and co-operation in tackling our joint problems. Perhaps we could start by considering a training scheme for Loading Bay personnel. Please let me have your comments and suggestions in writing by next Friday.

KL.

Skeme (Project)

NOTES ON THE MEMO
(Based on HI-FLITE)

A memo does not go outside your own organization. It can be in any form or style you consider suitable. Here, we shall assume that you are writing a fairly formal memo to someone who is not a personal friend.

Many organizations have specially printed memo forms, but a memo can also be written on plain paper.

LAYOUT

```
HI-FLITE STORES LTD         MEMORANDUM
From Transport Manager      To Loading Bay Supervisor
                            Date 30 April 1990

Subject Handling of furniture by untrained staff

1 It has come to my notice that in several recent
instances furniture has been damaged in the Loading Bay
because of careless handling by untrained or inexperienced
personnel.

2 Kindly ensure that in future all porters are
properly supervised at all times and that adequate means
are used to prevent damage to furniture after it has left
the sales floor.  All items leave the showroom in perfect
condition, and must be delivered in the same condition to
the customer.

3 I must comment once again on the unsatisfactory
relationship that appears to exist between porters and
lorry crews.  I appreciate the difficulties that these
staff face, but I do not believe they are insuperable,
given good leadership.  I shall appreciate your goodwill
and co-operation in tackling our joint problems.
Perhaps we could start by considering a training scheme
for Loading Bay personnel.  Please let me have your
comments and suggestions in writing by next Friday.

                                        KL.
```

Essential formalities. These are usually limited to *From – To – Date – Ref. –* (or *Subject –*). In our example, Landon uses job titles, but he could equally well use names:
From K. Landon
To Mr J. Bascombe
or even initials:
From KL
To JB.

Subject heading. This is nearly always a noun phrase. In our example, the headword is the verbal noun *Handling*; all the other words in the heading are dependent on it. A convenient way to make up titles or headings is to say first what general subject the memo is about, then what particular topic it deals with, for example: *Furniture: handling by untrained staff.*

The body of the memo. This should be in short, clear, simple sentences and paragraphs. Paragraphs are usually numbered.

Signing off. There is no farewell and no signature block. You simply put your initials below the text to show that the text is complete and that you take responsibility for what it contains.

LANGUAGE AND STYLE

Because Landon and Bascombe dislike each other, and because Landon is angry, this memo is written in an extremely cold, formal style. Even so, it is not completely impersonal. Bascombe will certainly become angry himself when he reads it; in paragraph 3, for example, Landon implies that Bascombe is not a good leader of the men in the Loading Bay. The vast majority of office memos, though often formal, are a great deal friendlier than this.

SECTION 3: A TELEX MESSAGE

NOTES ON THE TELEX MESSAGE
(Based on ELITE)

telex messages are less expensive to send than cables or telegrams, and the need to cut out every unnecessary word is not nearly so great. Nevertheless, time is still money, and a telex usually says what it has to say more briefly than a letter.

This is the telex Mr Kazumichi could have sent to Mr Thompson about the shortlisted candidates.

LAYOUT

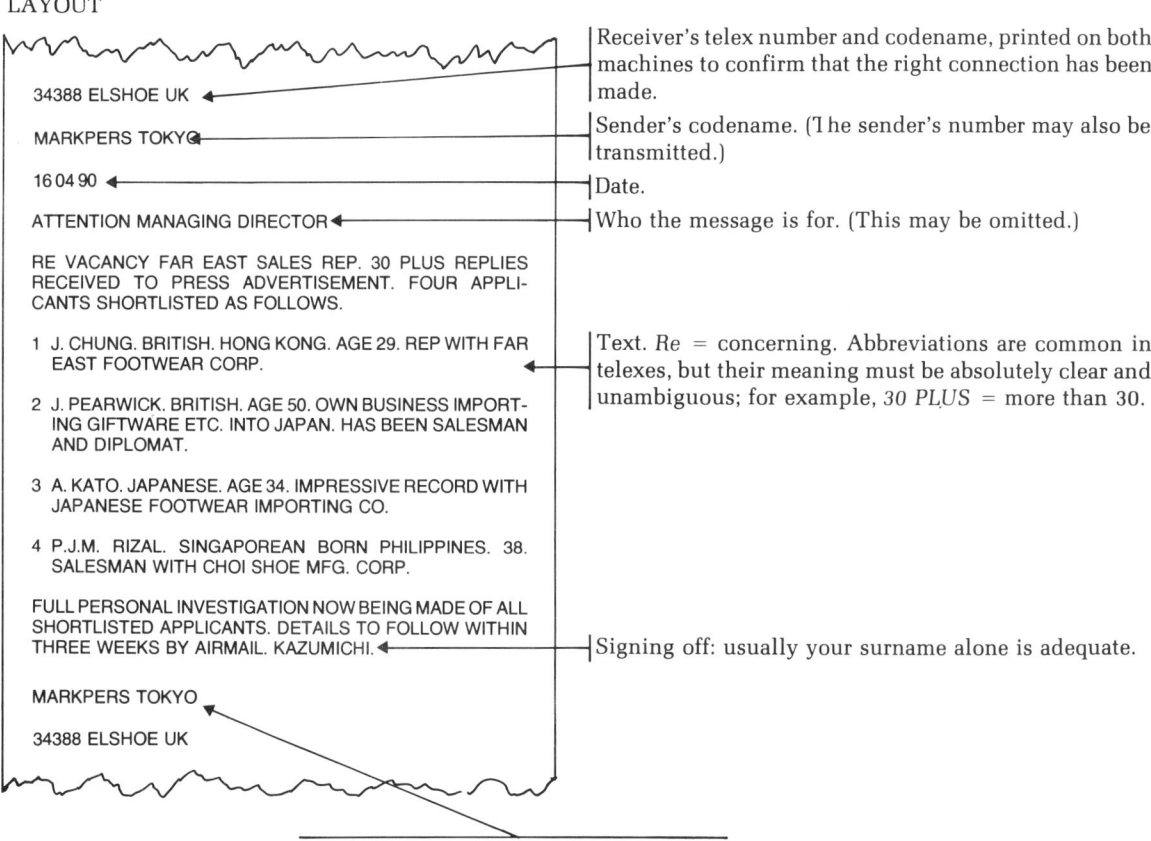

SECTION 4: A SHORT REPORT

REPORT ON SALES OF 'LIVEWIRE' FENCERS FOR YEAR
ENDING 31 DECEMBER 1990

1. As requested in your letter of 13 February, I am sending you a report on the decline in sales during the past year, together with my recommendations for reversing this trend. My findings are based on personal observation and experience of the Belgian market over the past five years.

2. Total sales and turnover for Belgium 1985-90 are summarized in the Appendix to this report. As you will see, they show a gradually accelerating decline in demand, and under present conditions no upturn is foreseeable.

3. The following factors appear to be operating to bring about this decline:

    (a) Overall reduction in demand. The market for electric fencers is, in some areas, almost saturated.

    (b) Increase in proportion of stock being kept under conditions of intensive rearing, with little freedom of movement.

    (c) Intensified competition from other manufacturers. Most of these are outside Europe.

    (d) Lack of awareness of JCS among Belgian farmers. Less than half of my first-time contacts have heard of JCS at all, and most know little or nothing of your products.

4. My recommendations are as follows:

    (a) Product diversification
    Two areas in which I believe similar product lines would do well are:

    i. zoos, particularly private zoos where animals are semi-domesticated

    ii. market gardens, where fruit and vegetable producers need to keep small animals out rather than in.

    (b) Price revision
    JCS fencers are superior in quality to the competition, but cannot undercut their prices. Customers who choose JCS therefore put quality first, and some have said they would pay up to 20 per cent above current prices.

    (c) Advertising
    A budget of about £3,000 would pay for a series of quarter-page advertisements in the agricultural press. This would help to overcome the problem mentioned in 3(d) above.

28.3.91   JC/mrt

NOTES ON THE REPORT
(Based on JCS)

This is Joachim Carpels's report to his Principal, following another disappointing year for JCS products in Belgium. Like all reports, it has a specific purpose—in this case, to help the Manager of JCS decide what to do. Everything in the report is chosen and arranged to serve that purpose as efficiently as possible. There is almost no irrelevant information; no time is wasted in telling the reader what he knows already. (Often, however, the writer does not know who his report will be circulated to; then, it may be necessary to give more background detail.)

LAYOUT

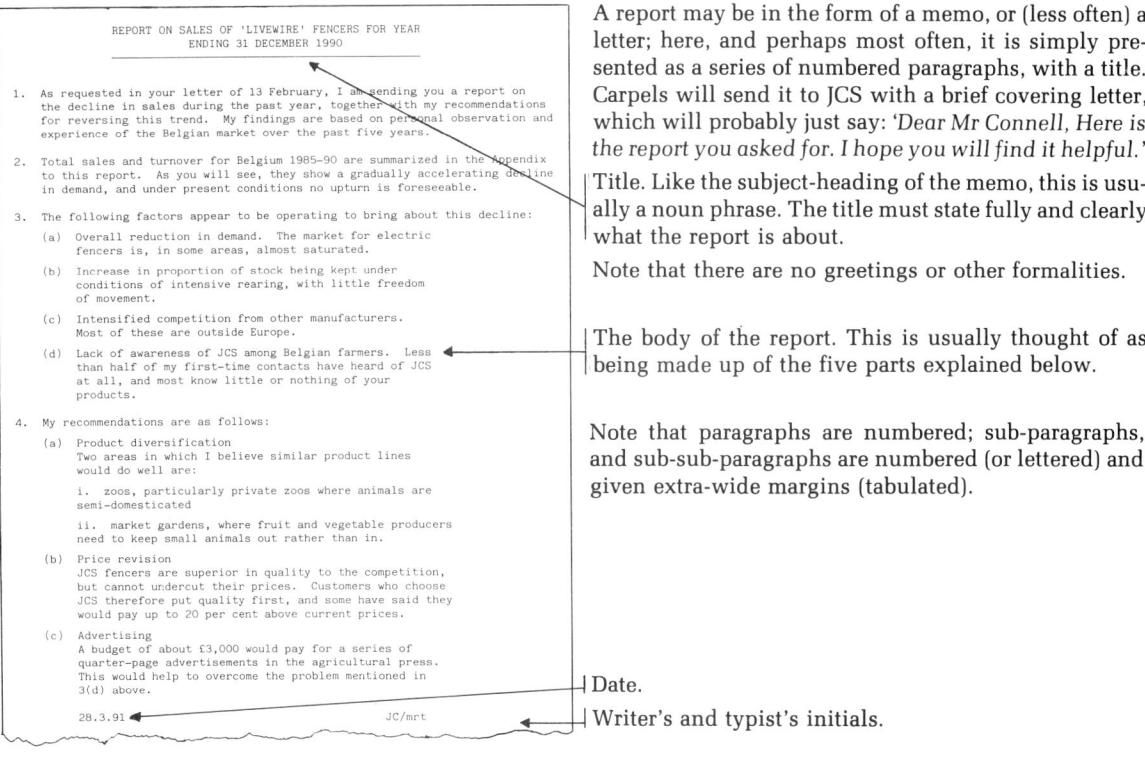

A report may be in the form of a memo, or (less often) a letter; here, and perhaps most often, it is simply presented as a series of numbered paragraphs, with a title. Carpels will send it to JCS with a brief covering letter, which will probably just say: 'Dear Mr Connell, Here is the report you asked for. I hope you will find it helpful.'

Title. Like the subject-heading of the memo, this is usually a noun phrase. The title must state fully and clearly what the report is about.

Note that there are no greetings or other formalities.

The body of the report. This is usually thought of as being made up of the five parts explained below.

Note that paragraphs are numbered; sub-paragraphs, and sub-sub-paragraphs are numbered (or lettered) and given extra-wide margins (tabulated).

Date.

Writer's and typist's initials.

THE BODY OF THE REPORT

The five parts of a typical report are as follows:

Terms of reference   This states why the report is being written and exactly what ground it covers.

Procedures   This part explains how the writer got the information that the report contains.

Findings   This part states the facts that the writer considers relevant and useful for his purpose.

Conclusions   These give your opinions about the facts.

Recommendations   These are the steps you believe should be taken. If you are not asked to give recommendations, or if they are obviously not required, then leave this part out.

These five parts are a framework for the writer to keep in mind while he is preparing the report; they are a guide to clear thinking, not a set of rules that you must follow slavishly. You may occasionally see *Terms of reference*, *Procedures*, etc. used as titles for paragraphs, but this is not very common.

In Carpels's report, the *Terms of reference* and *Procedures* are obviously contained in the two sentences of paragraph 1. Paragraph 2 contains part, at least, of the *Findings*. (Note that statistical tables and other similar detailed information are usually put in appendices to the report.) Paragraph 3 consists of both *Findings* and *Conclusions*. Carpels has not separated them because he considers this to be the clearest way of saying what he has to say. Paragraph 4 contains the *Recommendations*.

The use of numbers and letters makes it possible for people to refer quickly to any section of the report: thus, the recommendation about market gardens is in section 4(a)(ii). There are several common numbering systems, and Carpels's fourth paragraph could equally well be set out like this:

4
    4.1
        4.1.1
        4.1.2
    4.2
    4.3

Remember that a string of sub-paragraphs (like that in Carpels's Paragraph 4) forms a list of items. It is important that every item in the list should have the same grammatical structure as every other item. If the structure varies from one item to the next, the reader will find the list confusing and difficult to understand. In paragraph 4, for example, each recommendation is introduced as a single noun or noun phrase:

(a) Product ***diversification.***
(b) Price ***revision.***
(c) ***Advertising.***

Similarly, each factor in Paragraph 3 is explained in *the form of a phrase based on a noun:*

(a) Overall ***reduction*** in demand
(b) ***Increase*** in proportion . . .
(c) Intensified ***competition*** . . .
(d) ***Lack*** of awareness . . .